ENDORSEMENTS

Mr. Ramin Parsa has written an important book on how the ancient glory of Persia turned into ashes after Islam took hold of this great nation. Parsa's first-hand experience from living under Islam in Iran to embracing Christianity was a courageous and long journey that should help inspire us all.

Nonie Darwish
Author of "Wholly Different; Why I Chose
Biblical Values Over Islamic Values."

I have had the privilege of knowing Ramin Parsa for several years. He was a tremendous blessing when he ministered to the church I pastor, and the congregation looks forward to his return. Ramin and I have had many lengthy conversations and I can say with all my sincerity that he is one of the most genuine individuals I know. In a day when "political correctness" is the "norm," it is refreshing to see a young man who prioritises the truth that humanity so desperately needs, above the cultural pressure to conform to the vacillating standards of the day. I can assure you that the book you are holding will bless you with the uncompromising truths that embody the testimony of Ramin Parsa. "And you shall know the truth, and the truth shall make you free." John 8:32. This book, and its author, come with my highest recommendation. Be blessed as you read.

Pastor Chris Barhorst
True Life Church
Greenville, Ohio

Ramin Parsa has known, first-hand, the gross darkness of Islam from the inside out. He has also known, personally, the brilliant, saving light of Christ. His life was gloriously transformed by encountering the risen Lord Jesus Christ. God has raised up Ramin Parsa with a timely message that must be heard. This is a must-read book!

Joe Sweet, pastor
Shekinah Worship Center
Lancaster, California

We have known Ramin Parsa for several years and have done much ministry with him, both locally and during a trip to foreign nations in the northeastern Caribbean Sea. He is always conscious of the people who don't know Jesus, and is eager to lead them into a new life in the Kingdom of God. He is very well versed in the Bible and has an intimate relationship with the Holy Spirit. He has not lost his fire in an America that takes God for granted.

This book is the clearest presentation that I have ever read of the history, goal, and practices of the Islamic religion. It is a clear warning to America to beware of the insidious Islamic scheme to take over the nation by stealth, by using our own institutions of freedom against us. It is of the utmost importance to regulate and limit immigration from Muslim countries in addition to passing a law denying the implementation of Sharia law within these United States of America.

Ramin Parsa has sounded the warning trumpet, and has laid bare the plans of this enemy, which is masquerading as a religion. We must take this warning seriously and take action if we are to preserve our republic, our Christian faith, and the Constitution of our country.

Jack and Grace Tuls, missionary pastors
Remote Area Ministries
Lancaster, California

From ASHES to GLORY

THE TRUE STORY OF A FORMER MUSLIM FROM IRAN

RAMIN PARSA

WESTBOW
PRESS®
A DIVISION OF THOMAS NELSON
& ZONDERVAN

WestBow Press books may be ordered through booksellers or by contacting:

WestBow Press
A Division of Thomas Nelson & Zondervan
1663 Liberty Drive
Bloomington, IN 47403
www.westbowpress.com
1 (866) 928-1240

ISBN: 978-1-5127-9473-1 (sc)
ISBN: 978-1-5127-9474-8 (e)

Library of Congress Control Number: 2017911706

Print information available on the last page.

WestBow Press rev. date: 02/23/2018

From Ashes To Glory, is the story of an amazing young man, and a dear friend Ramin Parsa, who was born and raised a devout Muslim in Iran.

Mr. Parsa has a depth in knowledge of the Bible and a love for Jesus Christ that is beyond his age and I consider him like a son of mine ever since the day we met several years ago. Having been a former Muslim myself, like Ramin I understand his brave sacrifice when he openly declared his Christian faith before the world especially before the people and government of Iran.

Ramin converted from Islam to Christianity not after he moved to the US as I have done, but he believed in Christ when he was living in Iran, which is in itself was a miracle. I know that because I was able to believe in Christ after I moved to the US. When I lived in the Muslim world like Ramin I never knew Christ and could never dare touch a Bible, let alone convert to Christianity there. Doing that from over there would be a guaranteed death sentence.

Not only did Ramin convert to Christianity but he had the courage to start a TV show teaching Biblical values to the people of Iran. In fact when we first met Ramin invited me to be interviewed on his TV show and address the people of Iran. Ramin did make a huge difference through his TV show in the lives of many Iranians both in Iran and in the US as well.

What is unique about *'From Ashes To Glory'* is Ramin's delving into Iranian history of how this great civilization was taken over by Arab Muslims in the Seventh Century. In fact Egypt and Iran were conquered by the Arab/Islamic jihadist invasion in the same year of 639 A.D.

Ramin also talks about his horrific life experience under Islamic Law (Sharia), his struggles in his exciting journey to discovering the truth in Christ.

In this engaging and thought-provoking book, with depth and clarity, Ramin compares Islam vs. Christianity and their respective impacts on the world around us. Ramin helps and encourages the reader to an intimate relationship with Jesus Christ. He offers practical advice for leading Muslims to God's saving grace. This book reminds us to take heart because the simple but powerful message of the Gospel is healing and transforming the lives of people everywhere including the Muslim world.

Ramin's struggle to serving the Lord is at the center of his personal and his professional life. He is an important figure in helping expose the persecution of Christians in the Muslim world. He is also bringing the good news of Christ to the people of Iran.

Ramin is also a loyal and proud citizen of the United States and because of his love of this great nation he is bravely speaking to Americans about the challenge to Western freedoms and democracy from Islam and its barbaric legal system called sharia.

- Nonie Darwish

This book is the story of a former Muslim from Iran and his journey to a new life in Jesus Christ. He tells you the things he has seen and experienced while living under Islamic Sharia law in Iran. This book will consider the birth of Islam and its impact on people's lives in various nations, as well as the impact of Christianity on the world. You will also learn about the conflict between the West and Islam, Sharia law, Islamic jihad and how to reach out to Muslims with the Gospel of Jesus Christ.

CONTENTS

DEDICATION

I dedicate this book to my heavenly Father who has loved me unconditionally. He has known me since before the foundation of the world, and sent His only begotten Son to die for me.

To my Lord and Saviour, Jesus Christ, in whose righteousness I stand. After all, it's His story, the story of His redemptive grace, mercy, and the kindness He has shown me.

To the Holy Spirit who has graciously guided and taught me all these years. I couldn't do it without Him. He has inspired me to write this book. He is the one who has comforted me in difficult times.

And to my family, especially my mother, who worked so hard to raise me. Her love for God motivated me to seek the truth more fervently. She is an example of perseverance and endurance in hard times. She raised ten children in an oppressed and tough country. To my earthly father who didn't live long enough to see the glory days, but was diligently searching for truth.

To all my good friends who have helped and prayed for me tirelessly; to fellow ministers, brothers and sisters in Christ who have sacrificed so much to spread the good news of salvation. They believed in me, encouraged me, and taught me many good things. I'm deeply grateful.

And to the members of the persecuted Church, who are paying an unbelievable price to serve and follow the Lord, and the heroes of faith, those who are set apart for Christ's sake. Thank God for them. And to the ones who paid with their blood to serve God.

INTRODUCTION

I thank God that you followed His prompting to pick up *From Ashes to Glory*. My intent for writing it was to encourage you and show you an example of hope and resurrection in Christ. In addition, my aim is to expose Islam, compare its world impact and its values with that of Christianity, and share Christ's Gospel.

What humbly qualifies me to talk about Islam is the fact that I lived and breathed it for nineteen years, not in democratic America, but in war-torn Iran where I was born, just a few years after the hostile takeover of the Ayatollah Khomeini and halfway into the Iran-Iraq War of the 1980s. Raised in the wake of turmoil and oppression, I always clung to Allah, whom I longed to know and please but never could.

As I matured, my questions about life's meaning and purpose remained unanswered. This and other life events led to a painful awakening that I had put my trust in the furthest thing from a loving God. My arduous journey to Christianity was truly a rebirth, because as a Muslim and a non-Christian my spirit was dead.

Over the years and during my travels as a Christian evangelist both in the U.S. and abroad, people have asked me the same questions about Islam, the Christian faith, and the socio-political issues of our day. There is much confusion about Islam and why it has caused so much wilful strife, death and destruction anywhere it has dominated, for as long as humanity can recall. In the current climate of political correctness that undermines our very safety and that of our families, my aim is to shine a light on a deception, for beneath Islam lies an ideological threat to the West that is demonstrably real.

To move forward with purposeful clarity, we must understand the past, from both historical and Biblical perspectives. Therefore, in the following pages, I talk about the birth and spread of Islam, and how it reduced Ancient Persia's glorious empire to ashes. Leading up to Iran's modern history, I also delve into the centuries-long conflict between Islam and the West, the mission and plan of Islam, the intricacies of jihad and Sharia Law, that are seeping into our communities at an alarming rate.

Although I share my story of conversion in the opening chapters, *From Ashes to Glory* is not meant to be read as a novel, for each chapter thereafter offers what I believe to be valuable insights about the topics it covers, and can be treated as a stand-alone message.

If you are a Christian, this book will impart how to form a more personal and intimate relationship with Jesus and the Holy Spirit, and boldly share the Gospel with others, especially our Muslim neighbors who are mostly genuine but deceived and desperate for the Word of Life. May your hearts be stirred and your passion for the Gospel re-ignited. If you are of a different persuasion or none at all, I want to introduce you to God's abounding grace and love, by the power of the Holy Spirit, who has inspired me to write and share my story of hope and redemption, of rising out of the ashes and walking into Christ's glory.

Chapter One

I WAS BORN A MUSLIM

It was September 1985, in the thick of the eight-year Iran-Iraq war that started in 1980. I was born into a devoutly Shi'ite Muslim family in a village roughly sixty miles west of Shiraz, the capital of Fars (Pars), Iran, where the famed King Cyrus had his palace and his tomb is presently located.

According to Islamic tradition, my parents sang in my ears as a newborn in order to claim me as a Muslim for life. Shortly after that, I was circumcised which is a tradition they imitated from the Jews.

The revolution in 1979 effectively ended the Pahlavi Dynasty founded by Reza Shah whose successor was his son, Mohammad Reza Shah. My father was very much in favour of the Shah, but he lost his position and influence to the Muslim cleric, Ayatollah Khomeini, after the uprising. The Islamic Revolution produced the first Islamic government in the modern era, and early signs pointed to Khomeini's clear intent to export this type of Islamic rule to other countries.

I recall my father's stories about how the rebels and millions of people sang, "The devil leaves and the angel comes," as they pushed the Shah out of power and into exile. I also watched footages of the revolution on government-controlled TV. After Islam came to power, Iran immediately became hostile to the West. Muslims who were loyal to the cause of the revolution attacked the U.S. Embassy in Tehran, and held fifty-two American diplomats and citizens hostage for 444 days. Iran was placed under heavy sanctions because of this, killing all manner of tourism.

Mohammad Reza Pahlavi, the son of Reza Shah left Iran with tears during the islamic revolution. Mohammad Reza shah and his father served Iran well. Many countries refused to receive him due to political upheaval. He stayed in Panama for a while. Even President Carter was reluctant to allow him in the United States for medical treatment because he was concern about hostage crisis. Shah was suffering from cancer. Finally, after pressures from the president's aids, he allowed the Shah in for medical treatment and sure enough the Islamists in Iran attacked the U.S. embassy and took the Americans hostage. Later the Shah left the United States under pressure and the only person who was willing to receive him was Muhammad Anwar el-Sadat the third President of Egypt, serving from 15 October 1970. But this costed him his life, later Sadat was assassinated by the Islamists on 6 October 1981. Many believe that he was killed because he allowed the Shah to come to Egypt. The Shah was a close friend of Sadat. As result of Egypt receiving the Shah, the relationship between the newly founded Islamic regime in Iran and Egypt began to deteriorate.

Shah was a very close ally of the United States that protected the Interest of the United States and had stabilised the region. His ousted was a loss for the U.S. After the Islamic revolution, the entire region began to fight for their own Islamic revolution. Iran was also friendly to Israel.

Iran was an instrumental country for the West in order to send their aid to Soviet Union to be able to fight Nazi Germany.

My father's position about the revolution was quite clear. Friends, relatives and neighbours knew he opposed the Islamic regime; he was harassed and ostracised for his allegiance to the Shah. Islamists hated him.

Many thought that Khomeini's takeover would usher in a divine and holy government to establish the peace and justice that he had promised to Iran's people. Instead, the booming and vibrant economy that the Shah had previously established quickly turned to ashes in the hands of the Islamic regime. Newspapers, universities, and cinemas were shut down, guns were confiscated from the people, and women were forced to wear headscarves (hijabs).

Islam quickly gained supremacy, dominating the school system and every sector of society. The oppressive Islamic sharia law began to be implemented. People were told what to eat and drink, where to go, what not to do, etc. Many Jews who had come to Iran as refugees during World War II or those Jews whose ancestors had come to Persia centuries ago hastily fled to Israel or the U.S. Hundreds of thousands, if not millions, of important people left the country as they foresaw the terror that was soon to come and the decline that they were witnessing. These changes swept across the nation because Khomeini enforced Sharia law.

Whatever competed with Islam was diminished. Any form of recreational activities and entertainment became virtually nonexistent. News publications promoted Islamic values, which emphasised mourning, commotion and chaos. Hostile to the arts, Islam drove most of the artists and musicians out of the country, curtailing music and literature. Cassettes and video players became illegal, but people would secretly pass them around and swap records that they had owned from the Shah's time, or had obtained from outside the country.

Devices such as satellite receivers and dishes have recently been smuggled through the borders of Turkey and Dubai and sold in the black market. The regime controlled TV stations have been trying to prevent the public from viewing or listening to anything that opposes Islam, not wanting people, specially the new generation who had not seen nor experienced the freedom during the rule of shah to see the freedoms in foreign countries. But because people enjoyed no liberties whatsoever and were tired of the regime's systemic lies, they found ways to tune in to foreign programming to see how people lived on the other side of the world.

Khomeini's promise of utopia was a smokescreen. Over time, the majority of the people got undeniably poorer and poorer. Water, electricity, and other utilities didn't become free as Khomeini had pledged, but became far costlier than in any other country. The salaries of the teachers diminished and the costs of everything skyrocketed. In fact, Iran has the second richest gas resources and one-fourth of the oil wells in the world, but as of the date of this writing, an estimated 44.5%-55% of its urban population lives below the poverty level.

The Islamic government further mandated that no churches were to be repaired or built. Any form of opposition was not tolerated. People and groups who were perceived as threats were imprisoned, tortured, or killed. During that time and in the years that followed, thousands received the death penalty in courtrooms after mere minutes in judgment.

The Islamic regime in Iran executed 20,000 people only in 14 months. Their voices were silenced and the right to defend themselves, quashed. Many of them were important and influential dignitaries - parliament members, secretaries, pilots, engineers, doctors, and other professionals, whose only crime was they had worked for the Shah of Iran in the past. And they were the thinkers and the Islamic regime fared them..

The undercover massacres were carried out in the name of Allah. I had heard violent stories from prison workers who said that women political prisoners, whom the Islamic court sentenced to death, were raped before execution, if they were found to be virgins. Their captors believed that if they did so, those women wouldn't enter paradise. It was a time of desolation and great sorrow. But before people could express their revulsion against the new regime and its many injustices, a war broke out between Iran and Iraq, two formidable Islamic countries.

Ayatollah Khomeini was a muslim cleric as well as a critic of the Shah of Iran. He vehemently opposed the Shah and the Royal family. As result he was expelled to Iraq and then to Paris. From there he gave vicious speeches about the Shah and gave promises of a better Iran with many free handouts to people. BBC broadcasted his speeches through radio. Later in 1979, after Shah left, Khomeini returned to Iran. While on the AirFrance, he was asked by an aid about his feeling of returning to Iran and his answer was shocking to the people around him who helped and promoted him and thought he loves Iran but he replied: "I don't have any feeling." He really didn't care much about the country and the people as much as he cared about Islam.

The Lord showed me at the beginning of 2017 that the Iranian regime will soon fall, there have already been many protests and uprisings. It's like a volcano that is smoking and has the signs of an eruption. People are tired of being bullied by the Islamists. Inflation is skyrocketing. unemployment is at 12 per cent. Iran is known throughout the world not for its technological discoveries or economic achievements but for being the first sponger of terrorism. Just recently many people in various cities protest against the Islamic regime despite the danger of getting shot or getting arrested and tortured. There are many young people in Iran who are tired of the statues quo. People are fed up with 40 years of oppression and have nothing to lose anymore. In 2009 uprising a young woman named Neda was walking on the street and was shot by the Islamic regime and died on the spot. That incident caused an international outrage. The video went viral. As I am writing, people are protesting on the street right now. The Islamic regime is on the verge of collapse. For years the Islamic regime played games with people, they held elections just as a show to prove the western world that they still have legitimacy. They would put a hardliner in power, after they squeezed people then they would bring a "reformer" so people had to choose between bad and worse. This is to show the world that the Islamic regime still has favour with the people of Iran. They even would bring people from villages into the capital on the anniversary of the revolution to deceive the world with an image that was simply not true.

Those days are over. On December 28 2017 people came on the streets, without a leader, spontaneously in the a city the Mashahd. People were expressing their displeasure because of inflation and high costs of almost everything. This time people crossed the line and chanted: "Death to Ayatollah." and we no longer worship arabs." referring to Islam and Muhammad. Not only they rejected the regime but Islam as a whole. People also chanted "No reformer no fundamentalist, it's over." The protests inspired other cities to rise. President Donald J Trump also rightfully express his support to the Iranian people multiple times. Unlike Barak Obama who not only didn't support people in 2009 uprising but also sent multiple letter to Ayatollah Khameneie and struck a one sided deal which only helped the regime, lifted the sanctions and sent millions in cash to only be spend in sponsoring the terrorists. But that deal didn't benefit the people at all.

IRAN-IRAQ WAR

When Iraqi leader Saddam Hussein's troops attacked Iran, Iranians mobilised to drive them back to their country. A legion of willing fighters, many of whom under the age of eighteen, went to combat to protect the so called "divine revolution".

At the beginning of the war, the UN Security Council offered both countries the 598 Resolution, which called for a ceasefire, but Khomeini said, 'We want to conquer the world so that the world will become Islamic. We will continue until we take over Jerusalem. The more blood is shed, the stronger the roots of Islamic revolution will become.' Often, the regime took young people ages 13-25 to battle without their families' consent. The majority never returned home. If they would find male teenagers on the streets or in villages, the regime would take them by force to go to the battlefield. Families of these young men were not informed until these young men were killed in the battlefield.

The U.S., once a strong ally to Iran, became one of its most bitter enemies after the attitude of the Islamic regime toward U.S. and hostage crisis. As result the U.S. decided to aid Iraq. Other Western and Arab countries also got behind Iraq. The war lasted for eight years (1980-1988). During that time, more than one million young men perished and millions more wounded, as Iraqi forces bombed cities with chemical weapons. Many families lost five or six of their loved ones whose bodies were never found. The aftermath was devastating. Becomes of the incompetence of the Iranian regime, some parts of the war torn cities are still not rebuilt.

The war with Iraq essentially preserved the Islamic revolution in Iran because while the people were preoccupied defending their country, they lost sight of what was happening to their freedom. When the people saw that the revolution was failing, the regime aggressively spread the propaganda that the West was using Saddam Hussein in an attempt to abort and overthrow the new born Islamic revolution. The people became defensive and did everything to help the revolution, putting all sorts of props and supports underneath it, but it still failed. (Iranian revolutionaries confessed decades later that Iran actually provoked Saddam and the war that killed a staggering number of people could've been prevented.) "Martyrdom" and Jihad for the sake of defending the "Islamic revolution was promoted through monody and religious songs that emotionally motivated the youth to die for the sake of Allah.

I was only four when the war ended, but the turmoil in Iran was far from over. I was awakening to a nightmare. Eventually I started going to school where all the teachings were on Islam. Khomeini called America the "Great Satan" and mullahs (religious gurus) lined us up as children to curse Israel and America for being "evil." They gave us books that showed images of Israeli soldiers pointing guns at helpless babies and children, drilling into our heads that Jews and Christians were liars and that only Islam was the truth. We were too young to understand the words that we chanted: "Death to America! Death to Israel!" Little did we know that the darkest hatred for the West and Israel was being sown in our hearts.

Year after year, they forced us to celebrate the anniversary of the revolution. Those who didn't support the revolution were afraid to speak out publicly but privately criticise them regime. To strike fear in people's hearts, Islamists demonstrated the fate of people who opposed and spoke against the new regime. On my way to school at eleven years old, I saw public executions and bodies strung up on cranes out on the streets. Witnessing these things as a child made it nearly impossible to function normally. I couldn't eat or sleep for weeks. If I slept at all, I suffered from disturbing nightmares.

Chapter Two

MY LIFE IN IRAN

Having spent nearly two decades of my life in Iran, recently I began to realize my roots and heritage. The City of Shiraz was the actual capital of the Persian Empire centuries ago and one would be hard-pressed to find history, culture and poetry richer than that of Shiraz. Although a desert region, it's cultivated with majestic gardens, vineyards and flowers, which have their beginnings in the ancient Persian monarchs who loved gardening and wanted to be memorialized as gardeners. Images of magnificent blossoms throughout the city are seared in my mind as nearly every home had a tree or two in its yard.

There was no better time to enjoy a glass of faloodeh, a refreshing sorbet-like dessert with thin noodles mixed in with a syrup of sugar and rose water, than in the springtime, when the sweet fragrance of flora filled the air. Despite the destruction brought about by wars and social upheaval, the people of Shiraz are hospitable and warm, and some love of culture has remained in their hearts to this day.

As lovely as some of the scenery was, however, it's difficult to reminisce my growing years apart from the backdrop of constant chaos. I belong to the "Burnt Generation," aptly called so, as unrest was at its peak and war with neighboring Iraq was the focal point for many years. This sad reality is markedly true for most people who grew up in Iran's post-revolution era.

MY FAMILY

Tragedy struck our lives when my eldest brother was killed shortly after the revolution. He was a schoolteacher in an obscure village just less than a hundred miles from Shiraz. In the act of mediating between two rival groups, he was accidentally shot and killed. A bullet pierced his heart, exited from his back, and hit a woman behind him, killing her as well. Although I was born after he passed away, I learned from others that my brother was a righteous man who loved and served people selflessly. It was a devastating loss that my family struggled to overcome. In the midst of losing lands and experiencing harsh political persecution, my father's greatest sorrow was the sudden death of my brother.

But life went on. My parents kept busy making ends meet and raising six girls and four boys. It would take my parents a week to discover when one of us went missing! Our house in Shiraz was like a dormitory with three bedrooms and one bathroom (thank God the shower was separate from the restroom!). In our backyard were sour orange and walnut trees that my father grew. He would pluck the walnuts, take them out of the city, and plant them there. One of my older brothers and I spent many afternoons climbing a wall on one side of our property, secretly enjoying fruit off a neighbor's grapevines that had crossed over the common wall. A neighbor's lush and perfumed jasmine tree gracefully encroached on the opposite side of our yard.

I was "daddy's boy" up until the time I started going to school. He was my hero for his matchless skills in hunting, shooting and horse-riding before the revolution. I heard many stories of how brave and skilful my father was. One time he was attacked by three bears in the mountains. A mother bear and her male mate and a younger bear attacked my father and he had to defend himself and shot them. He was never proud of this incident and was remorseful. He felt bad that he had to shoot three beautiful animals but he had to.

My father faithfully fulfilled his obligation as a steady provider and I admired his resolute strength. Tough as nails, he was a serious man who rarely cracked a smile. Family, relatives and friends sought his wisdom and counsel in resolving disputes between individuals and groups. Erudite and gifted with a personality like Churchill's, he could easily have become a great politician.

My mother, the epitome of hard work and patience, kept our home in good order and prepared three meals for a dozen people day in and day out. My sisters helped, but the chaos seemed unceasing. Any peace and quiet that my mother enjoyed while all the kids were at school would come to a halt the moment we stormed home at the day's end, famished and sorely in need of showers. The madness would start all over again. Our evening routine consisted of quickly washing up, Islamic prayer, eating supper, doing homework, and getting ready for school the next day.

Families were generally larger during that time, so parents worked hard and rarely spent quality time with their kids. In our household, we figured out a way to do homework with little or no guidance because failing to do so would earn us a good whipping at school. On many occasions, however, when home life was less frantic, we would all sit together and listen to my mother's stories, which endeared me to her. She would later rely on me to help her with shopping and other duties.

My mother or sisters would ask me to go and buy some ingredients needed for a meal. I would walk on the narrow streets in summer or winter, raining or hot to but the requested item. On the way I would play and pick from people's houses oranges or grapes, depended on the season. I would arrive at the local store who had piled up many different vegetables and fruits. Fill my bag with what I needed and then go back home again. In those days we didn't have any digital or touch screen cell phones so we would enjoy the surrounding instead of sticking our head in a phone or tablet.

Every day the boys helped around the house and took turns buying bread from the neighbourhood bakery. We would go to the bakery and stand in a line to buy fresh and hot bread. You could smell the fresh baked bread from a distance.We did the same for milk but not as often. The milk was scarce and people had to go very early to find some. I remember walking down the street and catching a whiff of freshly baked goodies from a local store in the morning, or seeing the teahouses filled with people who had come from work at the end of a tiresome day. I'm the youngest son, so my brothers often weaselled their way out of chores and got me to do their bidding. I had no one else to cajole...or bully...into doing my menial tasks.

Besides the rudimentary chores and activities, the boys in the family spent a lot of time playing soccer. Almost every Persian guy has played soccer at some point. It was the only hobby we enjoyed as kids, but we could only afford to buy plastic soccer balls, so we had to improvise by cutting a ball halfway through and putting another ball inside. This way the ball would be heavier and wouldn't be blown by the wind as we played. Then we would use four stones to make two goals on the street, next to our house.

My brother and I, along with the neighborhood kids, would split in two teams and run after that crude ball on asphalt street, often kicking it too hard, far and high, and straight through the neighbor's window (consequently, we faced the wrath of our dads who grounded us for weeks)! One of our other cheap thrills was to ring the neighbor's doorbell and run away, dissipating any leftover energy. Smelly, sweaty, tired, and hungry best described us after long hours of playing in the hot sun on weekends.

The girls, on the other hand, were quieter and more reserved. They played with dolls and hopscotch, and helped with chores at home. That was all they did because the implementation of Sharia abruptly limited girls' activities in general.

My siblings and I bickered about different things, but we also cared for each other. I look back to the love we shared with bittersweet gratitude. One thing we all agreed on was my undeniable knack for impersonation. Because I noticed the smallest details in people's behaviors, I could mimic them to a T. If a guest came to our house, after he or she left I would talk and act like him or her on cue, and everybody would burst into riotous laughter.

I always wished I had learned to play some kind of musical instrument, but no such opportunity presented itself. Our toys and computer games were scarce and bicycles were beyond our reach, so our parents would take us kids to parks where we enjoyed passing the time. I also remember wanting to learn how to swim, but the school that offered lessons required students to first go through three months of studying the Quran. I went for a month and quit. The muslim mullah would seat there and read Quran out loud in Arabic.

One of my brothers who's a few years older than me had my back unreservedly. He was my best buddy and partner in crime. We got in trouble and invariably got punished together. One such instance was when we decided to skip school because our shoes were worn out from weeks of playing soccer (we didn't have soccer shoes). Our parents knew that we needed new pairs of shoes, but they were either too busy to remember or couldn't afford to buy them at the time. My brother and I were too embarrassed to show up at school in distressed footwear, so we thought it best to ditch our classes. However, one fine day, as we were loitering in the street, we ran into two of our older brothers who immediately questioned why we weren't at school. Our faces turned beet red before my brother could respond, his voice trembling, "But there's no school today!" One of them stayed put, as the other walked off to school to investigate. When he returned, he curiously agreed that there was no school, my brother and I were socked that is this a coincident?! but something felt terribly wrong. True enough, they took us home and gave us a bad whipping that we won't forget as long as we live. It's quite funny now, but back then? Not so much.

NORWOZ

It would seem odd that we never celebrated birthdays and anniversaries, but we were such an enormous family that getting past our daily routines and responsibilities was a huge accomplishment in and of itself. We did, however, celebrate Norwoz, a Persian New Year tradition, that starts the first day of spring. It's considered a time of renewal, of purging the old to make way for the new. Preparations typically began two weeks in advance. We would dust and clean the entire house, and my mother would ask me to take the heavy persian rugs outside, hang them over a wall and beat them with a stick. After the dust fell off, I would scrub the rugs with soapy water, rinse and then wring them. Finally, I would hang them over a wall again to dry.

We would go shopping for new clothes, shoes and a few items for the house. Elaborate cloths and seven symbolic items called Haft Seen or "he Seven Seens" would adorn our dining table or a big cloth on the floor.. For example, one of the items is a coin called "sekkeh" in Persian, which represents prosperity. We would also place a book (at that time the Quran) on the table. In some households, and mostly in recent years the Quran has been replaced with Divan-e Hafez, or Shahnameh, which were Iranian books of poetry. (Today, Christian homes use the Bible.) Other fixtures included a mirror with two candles, a goldfish in glass bowl (which I loved receiving as a present), a lamp, painted eggs, a bowl of water, wheat or bread, hyacinth flowers, some candy, and traditional confectionaries like shirini nokhodchi or nanberenji.

It was the most festive time of the year for families. Bakeries would be busy making all kinds of pastries and filling their stores with pistachios, almonds, and other seeds. We visited the homes of family and friends, and enjoyed wonderful food and customary sweets together. More importantly, it was also a time of reconciliation. People who had grudges or sour relationships found a way to lay their differences aside, visit with each other, and start over. As children, we also received "eidi" (money gift) from the adults and plus schools were closed for two weeks and kids had fun.

Chapter Three

ISLAMIC RITES AND RITUALS

Amidst fleeting episodes of quiet enjoyment with family, outside the walls of our home, the government went about its sordid business of using Islam to bring society to its heels. Public displays of Islamic practices ruled the day as the entire country became rabidly religious. I would see people on the streets beating their chests and shoulders to mourn their deceased religious leaders that were killed by other Muslims centuries ago. Wailing mourners were touted as "holier," especially those who wounded their heads with daggers and swords.

For as long as I can remember, I always hungered for God, and if rites and rituals were the way to please Him, I was going to learn and conform to all of them to prove my devotion. I understood that embracing all the traditions and customs of Islam meant I had to follow its commands as well.

As I matured, I willingly submitted myself to whatever Islam demanded. My family and I took part in all the Islamic festivals and temple activities. Fasting for the first time during Ramadan when I was eleven years old, I remember being so young and hungry that I broke my fast ten times on day one. I was so disappointed in myself because according to Sharia law, Muslims must not eat or drink anything between sunrise and sunset. After a while, though, I did learn to fast for days and weeks on end. That

I never felt Allah's love or presence had no bearing whatsoever on the job that was mine to do: yield to tradition and do what was expected of me.

I recall a time when a man ate food in public during Ramadan. He was beaten and penalized. The general notion is that when you eat food in public, people are tempted to eat as well, and therefore it's a sin. That's why restaurants are forbidden to sell food during fasting time. To this day, people cannot eat or drink water in public and food businesses must not serve patrons until after sunset, when the fast has ended and people have gone home. Many restaurants are forced out of business because of lost revenues.

At school, authorities also required students of all ages to fast. No one was allowed to bring any food. In addition, we had to memorize and recite the obligatory "Namaaz" (prayer) in Arabic five times daily during prescribed times, each calling for a specific amount of prayer. They forced these rituals on students because many resented participating, especially as we had to repeat the same words in a language that we didn't understand. This was necessary to go to heaven, we were taught.

As we advanced through every grade level at school, so did the indoctrination of Islamic values, to which most of us adhered out of fear. Any resistance or failure to obey was met with harsh correction. I remember a young man who was caught drinking alcohol, which is illegal and punishable under Sharia law. Police tied him to a bed in his neighbourhood and beat him publicly. A Quran was neatly tucked under the tormentor's arm as he punished the offender.

The fear and sadness that were embedded in my psyche didn't diminish my longing and curiosity for God, which only intensified well into my teens. Because Islam was the only option as it had pushed out all other rival faiths, I committed myself to learning and obeying the Quran. All government institutions had a mosque or prayer room. From the mosque at the Department of Agriculture where my friend's mother worked,

I would broadcast the call for prayer ("Azaan") over loudspeakers to communities within a three-mile radius.

Despite never seeing the faintest light of hope or feeling truly alive and loved, I persisted in performing all the rituals. Waking up at dawn, I would go to the mosque on foot, often braving rain or snow, just to pray from the core of my being. I would beat my chest and back with chains, weeping as I walked on hot asphalt to please Allah and earn points into heaven. I witnessed many other young people do the same, crying out in agony, in hopes that Allah would hear them and be pleased.

My family and I took part in many religious gatherings and ceremonies, most of which commemorated death and wars. We laid money at the shrines of dead imams (religious leaders), so we might get healed if we were ill, or to earn Allah's favor or an answer to prayer. Serious Muslims would chain themselves to the shrine to receive healing, but it was all in vain. No healing came. We spent an inordinate amount of time at gravesite of so-called Muslim saints, asking them to help us. But any money that my mother threw in the shrine came back void, as her prayers remained unheeded.

It always made me wonder why my mother who was a devout Muslim never ceased to ask for forgiveness in her prayers. I never saw anything wrong with her. In fact, she set a wonderful example by feeding and helping the poor without expecting anything in return. In my eyes, she was a saint and never did anything that could've deserved punishment. Perhaps somehow she knew in her heart that despite her good works, she wasn't quite in right standing with the Creator of the universe. Surely, others have the same feelings of dread and uncertainty about where they would go when they die, I would think to myself.

DOUBT AND DILEMMA

Much as I loved literature, poetry and history, school was more a place of terror than learning. Teachers beat us mercilessly when we neglected to do homework, or when we were caught not paying attention in class or even if we didn't do a good job on our tests or failed to solve a mathematic question. Often the teacher would right a math question and then ask different students to go and find the answer, if we couldn't answer it, we would get a slap in the face or smack in the head. or sometimes hit the palm of our hand with stick. Very Painful. We thought this was normal all over the world. If I close my eyes now and think back to those days, I can still see the fearful and pained faces of my peers. Students who were constantly hungry and intimidated couldn't study properly. The mandatory pressures imposed by Islam were so great that we just wanted school to be over and be with friends, many of whom harbored the same disappointment with the strict laws. The school would gather all the students in cold, freezing wether and read a passage of the Quran in Arabic and then forced us to chant "death to Israel and death to America."

As I learned more about Islam, I found it more challenging to accept its teachings. Every occasion of a missed ritual brought guilt and condemnation. I would see myself as defeated, imperfect, inadequate and inferior. On the other hand, if I had any measure of success in keeping the rituals, I would boast that I was better than other people. Either way, there was no assurance of heaven.

None of my own efforts quenched my thirst or led me to the true God. I never felt His presence. He was unapproachable, a being before whom I couldn't go. I feared Him knowing I wasn't perfect. I questioned whether the rituals that I diligently fulfilled day in and day out were enough. Feelings of inadequacy and shame never left me. It was difficult, if not impossible, to please Allah. All I wanted as a young person was to have a semblance of happiness and to enjoy life, but the religiosity of Islam and government oppression embittered me.

Many kids dropped out of school at a young age because either they lost motivation or were beaten and bullied by teachers or their families couldn't afford the steep tuition. Unfortunately, as it often happens among disenfranchised youth, many of the guys I knew wound up in jail for abusing and selling drugs. Prisons overflowed with young men, victims of needlessly punished families whose fathers were either jobless or addicted to drug.

Being entrenched in a culture of death and strife was dysfunctional at best. The lack of economic opportunity robbed millions of young people, just like me, of a future hope. But perhaps more egregiously, the stifling of self-expression and freedom beat us down. It was effectively slavery.

Society had been collapsing, so my parents were rightfully concerned about my future and that of my siblings. By the grace of God, we were firmly taught decency, and admonished to avoid all forms of evil. We could've easily ended up in drug addiction or crime, but God protected us. Our parents never failed to remind us to do well in school. Most of the parents were not prepare to face the new challenges because in their youth, they didn't have most of the challenges that their children were facing. Drug addiction, war, Sharia law, failed schools.

Meanwhile, my love of soccer early in life carried into my late teens. What used to be a distraction became a serious professional pursuit. I had enrolled to be part of a team, but they only accepted those who were part of the revolution or a para-military group called Basij. This group was at every mosque and controlled localities. Many teens signed up to earn certain privileges that enabled them to go to university or join a team. If you were a proven member of this Islamic groups called "Basij", then you would get many privileges such as priority to enrol at preferred schools and universities. This was one of the ways the Government used to lure young teenagers into the Islamic revolutionary groups.

A serious dilemma started to form in my heart because the deeper I got into Islam, the darker and emptier it got. But I also knew that walking away from the only religion I had known since childhood would be devastating. God was very important to me, and it was becoming painfully obvious that Islam didn't have the answers I was seeking, nor did it satisfy my hunger for a real encounter with God.

A TURNING POINT

The end of my allegiance to Islam could be traced back to a single event, the proverbial straw that broke the camel's back. When I was sixteen years old, my friends and I were going to a wedding. My buddies drank a small amount of alcohol (illegal under Sharia law) and I didn't, because I don't like alcohol in general. No one in the group was inebriated by any means, but what had started out as a fun and innocent time quickly turned into a horrifying ordeal that would change the trajectory of my life.

As we were driving in my friend's car, the police stopped us at a random checkpoint. Sharia law police often closed certain streets to check out cars and make sure people are keeping the sharia law. They immediately asked us to get out of the car and when they smelled the alcohol, ordered us to get on a bus filled with other young men who were also arrested for various petty crimes and violations. Within minutes, they drove us to a detention center where we were badly beaten for hours. They demanded we remove all our clothing, bar nacked, poured cold water on us, and struck us repeatedly with whips made of electric cables. We were humiliated as they mocked and laughed at us. It was one of the most crushing and degrading moments of my life. I was seething with rage at the inescapable punishment I was receiving for something I had no part in.

Then they rounded up fifty or so detainees and put us all in a filthy small cell that reeked of sweat and urine. We nearly choked in that small room that had no ventilation but for a tiny window. Twice a day, the guards would let us out for sixty-second restroom breaks, but if we exceeded our time limit, they would kick the bathroom door open. Between breaks, some of the men would relieve themselves in a bucket in the room's corner. In the days that followed, when the guards changed shifts very early in the morning, the new guard would do a roll call. If some of us were slow to respond (due to exhaustion) when our names were called, the guards would hit our heads with a baton. I was so broken, waking up with pain and rage and the feeling that I have failed my family. They treated us as if we were hardcore criminals. All they gave us for food were two eggs per day and water was in short supply. A big bottle that we passed around after taking a sap of water.

Whatever dreams and aspirations I had as a sixteen-year-old were extinguished in the blink of an eye. The despicable injustice that I was being subjected to, let alone for something I was not guilty of, dealt a massive blow to my already precarious view of reality. Even if I had been drinking alcohol, I shouldn't have been treated that way. Bitterness and anger quickly took root in my heart. I also saw the vastness of addiction and crime that had inflicted many young teenagers. broken Teenagers who were the products of a failed system and dysfunctional families and the islamic revolution had a big role in creating that mess. I saw many young guys in that jail that were suppose to be in school and at home with their families.

The courts were closed due to a religious holiday, so we were detained longer than anticipated. Days later, they took us to court with our hands and feet in chains and shackles where a religious mullah, who judged people based upon Sharia law, sentenced us to pay a fine. This was after our families had paid a bribe to reduce the punishment. Otherwise, we would've been slashed with whip on the streets. We were released after paying a hefty fine.

My recovery from that traumatic event took a very long time. I had been brutally victimized by Islam, a religion I was taught to embrace and respect. One might argue, "Well, that's not the real Islam; those people abused Islam." I beg to differ. What we experienced was a demonstration of real Islam, because they judged us exactly based upon Islamic laws. We were Sharia law violators and therefore Allah's enemies who deserved inhumane treatment. In cases where crimes commonly called for slashing with a whip, the enforcer would cling to a Quran as he carried out the sentence, often in public.

As if that wasn't painful enough, a couple of years later, my father passed away suddenly at 72. I remember it like yesterday. He was speaking to a group of people, quoting poetry, when he suffered a heart attack and expired shortly thereafter. Toward the end of his life, he began his search for God; where that took him, I don't know. One time I walked into his room and I heard him crying out to God as if he knew he doesn't have much time. About the same time, some of his former employees-turned-enemies who had joined the revolution also came to see him and apologized. They realized that they had made a grave mistake, but it was too late.

I was going to school and studying computer science at that time, but it didn't take long before I dropped out. I didn't have a sense of purpose and wasn't optimistic about my future in an unjust and rigged system. It seemed pointless to plan for a bleak life of no freedom. Why live through the next eighty or ninety years going to school, earning a degree, working hard, getting married and raising a family, all the while suffering in the hands of a harsh regime, and then dying? My outlook dimmed by the day. Beaten down by one hurtful event after another, I hungered for truth and meaning, but nothing could explain away my suffering or satisfy my questions about God. I had no desire to be with family and friends, so I left them and isolated myself.

As countless others before me have done, I, too, came to a point where I wrestled with certain questions. *Who is God? How did I end up here? Who created me? Why would a good God allow wars and fighting in the world? Why is a handful extremely wealthy whereas billions of people are mired in poverty? What about sickness and untimely deaths? Why are some children ill when they open their eyes in this world? Why is there no justice for those who are abused and persecuted?* And on and on.

Many Muslims believe that all things are fated by Allah. If someone broke a leg, it was meant to be. Each person's destiny - good or bad – is Allah's will. This didn't seem fair to me. Is it really Allah's will that millions of people in Africa suffer and starve to death? If Allah were real, He was either deaf or mute, or both. Not only that, but also the things that I saw in Islam, the violence, hatred and intolerance caused me to ask the question, could it be that Islam is false? My conscience was bearing witness that Islam is not divine but I had no other choice, I din't know anything else about God.

The more I thought about the meaning of life, the more depressed I got. The confidence that I had in the god of Islam was slipping away.

I was sure I didn't want to go on living in a world where my life was predestined and controlled by a group of immoral people. The disillusionment with a religion that failed to manifest a tight-lipped Allah weighed me down. I felt the worst pain in my spirit because God was the most important part of my life. Yet the questions persisted. *What's the purpose of creation? Who made us and why are we here?*

Days of neither sleeping nor eating turned into weeks. I wanted the pain to end. Like a virus, the thought of suicide gradually made its way into my consciousness. I saw life as nothing more than a gamble and there was no reason to go on. All that I had known and believed about Islam just crumbled beneath me, leaving a gaping hole of despair that I sank into almost willingly. The thought of taking my own life got more intrusive. I locked myself in a dark room where all I had were a TV and a computer. I was too enraged to even cry. Weak and powerless, my life had been reduced to ashes.

Chapter Four

MY RESURRECTION

Therefore, if the Son makes you free,
you shall be free indeed.
- John 8:36

One evening, as I was mindlessly flipping through the satellite TV channels, I stumbled upon a program host who was talking about Jesus. My knee-jerk reaction was indignant arrogance and outright refusal. I didn't want to entangle myself with another religion, let alone a Western version. Suspicious of most things, I wasn't about to trust anyone's empty words and claims. In my brokenness, I struggled with my dark past, the present despair, and an uncertain future.

The thought of living in a world without love was paralyzing, but at the same time I wasn't sure what would happen if I were to die. What afterlife would be waiting for me? Where would I go? Again, I was plagued with more questions: *If there is a God, why doesn't He help me? Why does He seem so far away and uncaring?* I couldn't blindly accept that atrocities were committed because of the teachings of Allah.

The urge to end my life intensified in the days ahead. Gazing at the TV screen like a zombie, I came upon the same preacher who talked about Jesus the week prior. Make no mistake…I was fed up with religion, but for some reason, I continued to hear the message. It was the first time that I truly listened to the Gospel and it was shocking to me. Something happened to me when I heard the words being spoken about Jesus. A light of hope decidedly shone on my heart. Then I had the most honest conversation of my life with my maker.

I was genuine in my appeal as I said these words from the bottom of my heart: **"Jesus, I don't know You. I was told You were only a prophet, but I'm now hearing You are the Son of God. I'm hearing that You died for me on the cross. I'm hearing that You went to hell for me and rose from the dead. I'm hearing that You are God who came in the world in the flesh. If this is true, I ask You to come into my heart, be my Lord and my Savior, forgive my sins and give me a new life. Help me, Jesus."**

Immediately I felt a holy presence in my room that was foreign to me. Suddenly, an indescribable heat wrapped around my left hand and traveled through my entire body. I was shaking, and the most peaceful and loving feeling overwhelmed me. I felt as light as a feather being blown by a gentle breeze, as if the world's woes and weight had been lifted off my shoulders and I could fly. Joy filled the dimmest crevices of my heart. I stood and jumped up and down, knowing without a doubt that it was God. I felt love. I felt an amazing sense of love. Somehow, I knew this was the truth I had been looking for. I began to thank God and praise Him for His goodness.

Then utterance of a beautiful language I had neither heard nor spoken before, formed and flowed out of my belly through my mouth. It didn't sound like a known language. **For years, I prayed to Allah and never got an answer, but the first time I called upon the name of Jesus, He heard and answered me!** At nineteen, I had just received the best news a human being could possibly hear.

Shortly after, I went to my mother's house, and as soon as she saw me, she exclaimed, "Your face is shining! What happened to you?" I said, "I gave my heart to Jesus!" as she had been sick for years, I then laid my hands upon her and commanded that sickness to leave. I had never seen a Bible and I didn't know I needed to rebuke the disease or lay hands on her. It was the Holy Spirit guiding me and she was healed. Praise God!

Reflecting upon my mother's long years as a fervent Muslim, I had seen her pray and weep for Allah's forgiveness more times than I care to remember. But after experiencing a healing miracle in her own life, she later gave her heart to Jesus. This time her sins were washed in His precious blood. Salvation had come to our house! I believe God was merciful in hearing my mother's prayers all along and He answered them when we found Jesus. See, God is one and He knows everything. He knew my mother and I were genuine but we were going the wrong path. Once we found Jesus and received forgiveness and salvation then God was able to bless us.

Ever since then, I slept like a baby and my appetite returned. I prayed non-stop and talked to Jesus every moment that I was alone…while walking, before going to bed, as soon as I opened my eyes in the morning. He became everything to me. I was so enamored of Jesus and caught up in conversation with him that I didn't notice the passing of time.

I maintain that the precise moment I came across the TV preacher was no accident. God had orchestrated it. The change in me was immediate, as if I was injected by a powerful, life-giving serum that reversed the symptoms of a disease and revived my dying spirit. I wanted to forgive my worst enemy, and felt compassion toward others, even those whom I used to hate. I knew I had become a different person on the inside. I don't claim to be perfect, but I know Jesus changed the person that I was. My perfection is from Him. I was born again, forgiven all my sins, and filled with the Holy Spirit. I had entered a covenant with God.

This time I could feel that my prayers are not in vain. I had assurance of salvation that if I were to die, I had the confidence to go to heaven without a doubt. I had a purpose for life, to herald the good news of the Gospel of Jesus Christ to a desperate and hopeless world, it brought me joy when shared the Gospel with people. I lived to unveil the riches of His grace. I had such a joy that it seemed God was smiling as I was doing the right thing.

Instantly I started searching for a Bible. I knew Christians had a holy book, but I had never seen it. I visited store after store and combed the city's libraries, but couldn't find one. For three months, I searched. Some said it was illegal. Others opined that the Bible was "corrupted".

So I tried the Internet, which the regime purposely kept agonizingly slow. Authorities didn't want people to access any potentially "dangerous" (meaningful and eye-opening) information, let alone have it be at their fingertips. In fact, when I searched for the word "Enjil" (the Gospel) and waited a great while, an ominous message came up on my computer screen: "Access to this website is prohibited." Naturally, I put my curious computer science skills to the test and rather easily circumvented the blockage by using the proxy system on my computer. I suppose frustrated people get quite savvy and resourceful under dictatorships that want to limit and stifle them!, I stumbled upon the Gospels of Matthew, Mark, Luke and John, but I also saw Acts, Romans and Corinthians. I wondered about the long list of names. The only thing I knew was Enjil which means Gospel and I saw four of them, I thought there was only one book?! Thankfully, I was able to download the four Gospels.

From morning to night, I read the good news and wept uncontrollably. I couldn't understand why this book was illegal, for in its pages were instructions to love and forgive one another, honor our government leaders, and pray for them. I read Jesus' words about rendering "to Caesar the things that are Caesar's, and to God the things that are God's." Why was this book's message of hope and peace forbidden from touching the hearts of millions in my country? The Words of Jesus were so strange to my eyes and ears. They moved me deeply. I had never heard anyone say, "I AM the resurrection and the life. I AM the Bread of Life. Let not your heart be troubled. Love one another. He who believes in me will not perish."

These words comforted and refreshed my spirit. It gave me such a sense of home and certainty. Jesus was speaking with authority, with assurance. He was bold and courages. There was no fear or doubt in His tone. I loved His message. It accompanied with signs and wonders, healing and miracles. It seemed too good to be true, but I already had tasted His power and glory. It was undeniable. Now I know why we have four Gospel in the Bible. Four different people witnessed Jesus' life, His miracles, teachings, death and life and testified about it, some of which even gave their lives for being a witness for Jesus. Luke who was a physician researched and wrote about the birth, life, death and resurrection of Jesus. the Words of Jesus were powerful, convicting and convincing.

I was troubled to learn how He was killed. But the narrative went on to describe that He rose and conquered the grave. Because He defeated death, I didn't need to be afraid anymore, for it's only a transition. 1 Corinthians 15:55 read, "O Death, where is your sting? O Hades, where is your victory?" Because Islam focused on death, defeat and hatred, these new Words were no less than revolutionary to me. These were messages of redemption, victory and hope! I felt I was being washed clean.

Some critics have said to me, "You are brainwashed," to which I respond, "Yes, my brain needed a lot of washing. I believed wrong, thought wrong, did wrong, and I needed a washing!"

As I continued reading the Gospels, tears of joy ran down my face. Then I thought of many young people like myself that were hopeless and desperate for whom I quickly made copies on CD and handed them out at the gym. All were seeking hope! On one occasion, as I was talking to someone about Jesus and the Gospel, a few young men overheard our conversation and approached me asking, "Can we have a copy as well?" I was delighted to help them all.

Days turned into weeks and seasons changed. My intimacy and relationship with Jesus grew stronger. I was in love with Him, incessantly seeking, worshiping, and acknowledging His presence at every turn. I meditated on his Word. It was as if I was walking on clouds.

Several months later, a stranger with a long, yellow beard and a long knife attacked me while I was at a phone booth minding my own business. I didn't know him and he acted like he was demon-possessed. He hit my head and arm with the knife, and as I fell backward, my leg went up and he stabbed it. He got in his car and sped away.

Right then I knew I had to leave the country. I wanted to grow in my faith, but I didn't have a church to attend, or a pastor to guide and mentor me. The environment wasn't safe anymore. The forces of darkness were marching against me, and I felt the Holy Spirit was prompting me to make a move.

Days later, I was at a crossroads and after much prayer, made a decision that would redirect my path forever. It was time to go. I didn't tell anyone of my "departure plan" because my mother wouldn't have let me go. No arrangements awaited me. No distant relative was expecting or picking me up at some predetermined location.

I grabbed a few clothes and the $300 I had saved, threw them in my backpack, and got on the road. As I walked farther away from home, I took one last look at the neighborhood I grew up in. knowing that I wouldn't be making my way back there for at least a long time. The one thing I was sure of was that the Lord was with me. His presence was my confidence and assurance. A nineteen-year-old was leaving his homeland and embarking on a new adventure.

Chapter Five

AN URGENT ESCAPE

Not knowing where I was going, I just trusted and obeyed the Lord by faith. I made it to the bus station and got a ride to an area close to Turkey's border. Without a passport because in Iran men have to serve in the military for two years to get a passport and women have to get a permission from their father, husband or brother., it would be almost impossible to leave the country, especially across that sensitive border. I didn't have a hard copy of the Bible, so I wrote many Bible verses on a piece of paper and read them to encourage myself. I memorized several other verses and muttered them under my breath often. Some of the verses were as follow:

Let not your heart be troubled; you believe in God, believe also in Me. John 14:1

"And whatever you ask in My name, that I will do, that the Father may be glorified in the Son." John 14:13

Without the Word of God and its encouragement, there was no way I would have succeeded. The pressure was so intense that my soul would have been crushed had it not been for the Holy Spirit's abiding strength and guidance. Such a great impact the revelation of the Word of God has had on my life. The Psalmist said it best in Psalm 119:105: *"Your Word is a lamp to my feet and a light to my path."* The Word was a lifeline that completely transformed my thinking and gave me hope to keep pressing forward, day after day. So many truths were hidden from me before. No wonder the devil hates the Word and fights it with all he has. The Word brought illumination and revelation.

By a miracle of God's grace, I was able to cross the border and found myself in Turkey. I crossed mountains, rivers, valleys and villages. I cannot mention the details of how it happened, for the sake of others' safety. The odds were stacked against me, but I quickly learned that Jesus makes a way when there doesn't seem to be one. One time I was very close to be arrested but God in His great mercy protected me.

One of the people I met while crossing the border found out that I didn't have any friends in Turkey, nor a clue where I was heading. He suggested the part of town where I might find some Persians. This man appeared to be a drug addict and my heart went out to him. I could tell he was embarrassed when I saw him smoking opium during one of our stops, but I only felt compassion and concern for him. Although he was fleeing a chaotic country, he was imprisoned on the inside. I shared the Gospel and told him how much Jesus loved and cared for him, and that Jesus could help him break free from his addiction. He listened, but didn't commit to the Lord at that moment. I was sure God wanted me to sow a seed into that man's heart, so the Holy Spirit could use those words to convict and eventually save him.

Not knowing any Turkish, I was completely relying on the Lord to help me. I reached the area that I was advised to go. When I heard a man speaking Persian, I approached him and, according to my custom, asked if he knew Jesus. "No," he replied. We talked for a while and he said, "But I'm going to a church to see what the Christians believe. Would you like to go with me?" I learned he was also an immigrant whose wife and children were already in Liverpool, England, and he was eagerly awaiting his visa so he could join them. He hadn't seen them in a long time.

Later on, I realized that Persians rarely shared details of their personal life to strangers, so they wouldn't get arrested if they returned to Iran. The Islamic regime would send agents to spy on Iranians in other countries. People hid their identities so they couldn't be reported to border authorities. But the Lord gave me favor with people, and somehow the Lord moved them to assist me. They would go out of their way to do so. I knew this was all the grace of our Lord Jesus Christ.

I was so excited to go to a church for the first time in my life. My heart was pounding. I felt I was going to God's house, and I was! The Bible says: "you also, as living stones, are being built up a spiritual house, a holy priesthood, to offer up spiritual sacrifices acceptable to God through Jesus Christ." Not only each of us Christians are a house for God but also our corporate gathering is where God is and each one of us are a living stone building a living house for God to dwell .

As we approached a building, I heard singing and shouts of joy in Persian. It was unlike any religious experience I had before, as Islam does not appreciate music. This time people were singing and praising God whose presence was strong among them. It was the most beautiful feeling of my life, as if I was giving my heart to Jesus all over again. I felt that I belonged there, like someone had been waiting for me all along, and that I had finally come home. I felt that I now those people for years and I didn't feel like a stranger at all. I felt connected to people and fit to be there. It was holy brotherhood. It was amazing.

The church pastor warmly welcomed me. And asked if I am a believer. He asked how I came to know Jesus, and I couldn't wait to tell him and others my story! They all praised God for my salvation. The people were so cordial and sincere. A church member invited me to his home where I stayed for a few weeks.

The man who took me to the church gave me the first hard copy new testament. I was so happy and grateful. But I had to see if it was the same as what I had previously found online and read. Praise God, it was the four Gospels, Acts, Romans, and all the epistles, plus Revelation. It was as if someone gave me the whole world! I held that New Testament close to my heart, not wanting to lose it. I didn't want anybody to take it away from me.

As I would sit in a bus or sitting in a park, I would open it and read from it, before I realise it, I would be lost in its glorious power. I read and read and read, memorised verses, prayed and meditate on the Word of God, even as I am writing, I burst into tears when I remember those days. It was as the Word of God was my only close companion, my partner. It wasn't like any other book, It was like a person walking and talking with me. I would sit and read at bus stations or while I was waiting somewhere. Later, the church gave me a complete Bible.

So hungry and on fire for God, I went to all the church meetings every day. Bible studies, youth group meetings, women's meetings, etc.! I met some people whose dedication moved me, for they would walk five or six miles, carrying babies, to attend these meetings. The church service was at 5:00 PM. The service lasted two ours and then we had fellowship and drinking some hot Persian tea and afterward we cleaned the church. By the time they were leaving, it would be around 10:00 or10:30 PM. The nights were dark and cold, no cars or means of transportation. Streets were dark and quiet except frequently hearing stray dogs bark. The cold weather didn't stop them, neither did the risk of being arrested. They all had to rely on God's goodness and protection, more so because I was in the country illegally, and my regular attendance put the church at risk of being shut down or harassed by disorderly locals.

Some refugees and immigrants who had converted to Christ often found it difficult to make a public confession of faith, as they feared for their safety and that of their families. Six months later, the man who accompanied me to church, called from Liverpool to share that he was reunited with his family, and that he was a brother in the Lord now! I was pleased to receive the news and grateful that God saved him.

Life in Turkey was not too easy, extremely cold winters, shortage of electricity and gas made things more difficult. Buildings didn't have any sort of insulation. Inside the buildings were extremely cold during the winters and hot and humid during summers. The only thing on the streets in winter was ice and snow. We had to fill empty oil barrels with water, insert a bare electric cord at midnight until morning to warm the water so we could take shower. We did so because we didn't have any other heating system. We had to do it at midnight when most people were sleeping and electricity was stronger then. During winters, because people used electricity so much, that sometimes the whole city would blackout.

Turkey is in shortage of energy. The most common source of energy was electricity but the source could not support so many people. There were nights that I slept in freezing cold concrete rooms. Even three or four blankets were not sufficient to keep me warm. Sometimes because of extreme cold I had to wear multiple socks the entire week. But despite all these difficulties I was joyful, Jesus was my hope and His presence in my life gave me peace. His Word gave me so much hope and faith. Holy Spirit comforted me and I was often praying in the spirit and reading the Bible. We shared our goods with each other and if someone was in need, we would rush to help.

We had prayer meetings and Bible studies every single day of the week. Not religiously and out of obligation but diligently and joyful. After work, in the evening, we would gather at any of our church member who had volunteered to host us that evening. We would sing worship songs and praise the Lord fervently with a few songs as a member played guitar then pray, study the Bible. Afterward we would drink Persian tea and home made cookies. The church was the only healthy, hopeful and joyful place. We would sing songs as we walked back home on dark, cold streets covered with snow. We would hear our steps as we stepped on fresh snow.

As I was in the country illegally, friends from church advised me to apply for refugee status. I went through a strict process, and after almost a year of waiting, by God's grace, my application was finally approved and I was accepted.

Meanwhile, the church congregation was growing rapidly. Many Muslim Kurds, Turks, Afghans, and mostly Persians - were converting to Christ. Soon the building could no longer contain the large group. We tore down concrete walls to expand the space and accommodate more people. We didn't have hired workers, it was us, the church members. One day, as we were doing construction work, a Muslim man walked by and asked what we were doing. One of our church members who didn't speak much Turkish said only one word, "Kellisa," meaning church. The Muslim man left, and within an hour came back with a mob who angrily threatened us, "We will kill you because you will corrupt our children! We will bomb your church! We don't want you here! You are infidels!"

I wondered why the community of self-righteous didn't condemn a disco with a bar that served alcohol not even a mile from our church. Yet in their eyes, honoring and following the true God was offensive and warranted insults and violent threats.Within a few minutes, the police and secret service showed up, media rushed to the scene, and instantly it was chaos. The police said, "They will harm you, you must stop immediately." We halted our activities and had to find another place and move to another house, where we started all over again. We worshiped silently and covered the windows with cloth to muffle our songs and praises. But it still wasn't safe, not to mention extremely cold. We kept warm by burning coal or wood in a stove. After some time passed, we continued our construction at the first building, but secretly at night.

Over the next few months, I was arrested four or five times for passing out Bibles and tracts, and for preaching the Gospel on the streets. The police chief called me in, cursed and yelled at me, and his underlings threatened to deport me. Had i not applied for refugee statues, I would have been deported on the spot. Although the Turkish government was supposedly secular, Muslims governed it. Legally, based upon Turkish constitution

I had the right to actively share the Gospel and worship freely, but in reality, they enforced their own Islamic laws.

An agency had given me a phone number to call, so I could find out which country I would be sent to. I was told that I was going to the United States! I went through a tough vetting system that included a few interviews and a medical examination, etc., later realizing that others had spent between five and twenty-five years in Turkey as they had failed to go to another European or Not American countries. Naturally, I was humbled and grateful. I knew this too was God's grace above all else that the Lord had done in my life.

After two years in Turkey when I was preparing to leave Turkey, I couldn't wait to put all the persecution and difficulties behind me. I had learned many things there and had been very close to the Lord despite troubles, but I was excited to move forward with God's plan for my life. Days later, however, as I sat on the plane waiting for it to take off, I felt the Lord speak to me very strongly: **"Be careful that you don't lose your fire when you get to America!"**

I was perplexed by the Lord's message, but didn't give it much thought at that time. Meanwhile, I shared the Gospel with the African-American woman who sat next to me. She was returning to Los Angeles, and I was eager to share my testimony during our time together, but she said she wasn't interested. Up until that moment, I thought everybody in America was Christian and went to church. This was my first glimpse that the Christian faith is being taken for granted in some places, whereas it's the most valuable treasure and the only hope for people in others.

Weeks later, I came to understand what the Lord meant when He spoke to me. America can be a dangerous place for faith because the people have it so good. Quality healthcare, excellent hospitals, abundance of food, education, clean water, welfare system and many other entitlements. There is a tendency to depend on God less and overlook Him as the source of all good things.

Chapter Six

MY NEW COUNTRY THE
UNITED STATES OF AMERICA

As arranged by the U.S. Government, I stayed a night in New York en route to Oklahoma, with a stopover in Texas. I came to America with $100 in my pocket. When I arrived at the airport in Tulsa, I knelt down to thank and praise the Lord for the blessing of a free land! I knew America was now my home. I considered it an honor and a blessing from the Lord and I wept for joy.

As planned, I stayed with a Christian brother and his family for nine days. He showed me around and took me to church. I would often be overcome with joy and gratitude to be able to worship freely and without government intrusion and seizure.

However, I was surprised to come across so many people who criticized and blamed America for the world's problems. Have they forgotten what a blessing America is to other nations? In cases of natural disasters, American Christians are the first to respond. In cases of international unrest, the U.S. brings peace and relief, defending the oppressed and causing dictatorships to fall. America has opened its doors to many who have fled violence and persecution in foreign countries. Most people don't appreciate what they have until they lose it. Although our hope resides in heaven and our home is beyond the blue, I'm not ashamed to join many other thankful people in singing, "God bless America, the land that I love, stand beside her and guide her through the night with a light from above. God bless America, my home sweet home."

After some time passed, I began to share my testimony at different churches. God gave me many good friends with whom my ties were tight and genuine. When I got my own apartment, a pastor named Todd and his family brought me furniture, utensils, and other supplies, etc. I met them through Mark and Jan, whom I befriended while they were on a mission trip in Turkey. To this day, we are like a family. I will never forget the love and kindness that they have shown me, a virtual stranger. It was hard to leave my family in Iran at a young age, but the Lord delivered on His promise to His children, as He said to Peter:

> Mark 10:29-32:
> *Then Peter began to say to Him, "See, we have left all and followed You." So Jesus answered and said, "Assuredly, I say to you, there is no one who has left house or brothers or sisters or father or mother or wife or children or lands, for My sake and the gospel's, who shall not receive a hundredfold now in this time—houses and brothers and sisters and mothers and children and lands, with persecutions—and in the age to come, eternal life. But many who are first will be last, and the last first."*

Indeed my friends grew in number and God continued to arrange many divine encounters. I remember a church where a precious woman was healed of breast cancer, after I simply shared how great Jesus is and how He healed my mother of her illness. One especially profound encounter was with a sister in the Lord who told me about Bible college. When I was in Turkey, I had a dream that I was in a huge Bible school with hundreds of other students. I knew the call on my life was to serve the Lord and His Gospel. I had a strong desire to further my study of the Word and become better equipped for service.

My friends invited me to a special camp meeting at a church that also had a Bible college. When I got to the meeting, I immediately knew in my spirit that this was the college the Lord wanted me to attend. It was Rhema Bible Training College. I remembered the dream I had while in Turkey. I was so blessed that the Lord opened the door for me to attend Rhema.

Time does not permit me to tell you all the ways that the Lord Jesus has been faithful to me. He is so awesome and wonderful! Jesus is my best friend, my hero, my rock and fortress, my salvation and hope! Jesus is my everything. I cannot imagine how I could live apart from Him. As the Psalmists said, His love is like the cedars of Lebanon, His faithfulness like Mount Zion. His goodness is everlasting. He is merciful and gracious. He has carried me in His hand. He has nourished and cherished me as a good father would his son. He has healed my heart. He has restored me. He has compensated for everything my family or others couldn't do for me, and everything the world took away from me. How could I not serve Him? How could I not love Him? How could I be ashamed of Him and His Gospel? His love melts a stony heart. Jesus, Jesus, Jesus, my love, my hope, my joy! How could I not bow down and respond with less than unbridled gratitude to the name above all names?

When I opened the Bible for the first time, I entered a whole new world. I read the four Gospels again and the words were almost bizarre to me. As it were, I was a parched tree in the middle of a scorching desert and suddenly life-giving water flowed into the roots of my Spirit. Sometimes we in the West take for granted the blessing that the Lord has given us. People have so many Bibles, translations, and tools that they treat the Word of God like a valueless thing. People around the world are desperate for these words. The world is looking for a Savior. Jesus is the Hero, the Savior. I had never heard such beautiful and powerful words like:

*Matthew 5:43-48: "You have heard that it was said, 'You shall **love your** neighbor and hate **your** enemy.' But I say to you, **love your enemies**, bless those who curse you, do good to those who hate you, and pray for those who* *spitefully use you and persecute you, that you may be sons of **your** Father in heaven; for He makes His sun rise on the evil and on the good, and sends rain on the just and on the unjust.*

John 11:25-27: Jesus said to her, "I am the resurrection and the life. He who believes in Me, though he may die, he shall live. And whoever lives and believes in Me shall never die. Do you believe this?"

She said to Him, "Yes, Lord, I believe that You are the Christ, the Son of God, who is to come into the world."

John 14:16: Jesus said to him, "I am the way, the truth, and the life. No one comes to the Father except through Me.

Mathew 11:28-30: Come to Me, all you who labor and are heavy laden, and I will give you rest. ²⁹ Take My yoke upon you and learn from Me, for I am gentle and lowly in heart, and you will find rest for your souls. For My yoke is easy and My burden is light.

*Luke 12:32: Do not **fear, little flock**, for it is your Father's good pleasure to give you the kingdom.*

John 3:16-17: For God so loved the world that He gave His only begotten Son, that whoever believes in Him should not perish but have everlasting life. ¹⁷ For God did not send His Son into the world to condemn the world, but that the world through Him might be saved.

John 1:14: The Word became flesh, and dwelt among us and we beheld His glory the glory as of the only begotten of the Father, full of grace and truth.

Oh how these words revived my spirit! They were not the words of career politicians with self-serving interests, nor words from false advertisements .nor empty, sophisticate words of a philosopher but rather simple but deep and powerful Words of the Savior.

One day I went to Walmart and I could hardly believe my eyes! A stack of Bibles was right in front of me! My heart was stirred because I remembered the long months I was looking for a Bible in Iran where it was illegal to own one. And there I was staring at a heap of Bibles in a retail store. People walked by the table, paying it no mind, while my eyes widened like a kid's would in a candy store! Thank God for freedom! Thank God for giving birth to America, where I can worship freely, and I can carry my Bible without the fear of government meddling. Oh how sad that people don't appreciate what they have.

It didn't take long before I started working for the Trinity Broadcasting Network where I learned many things that helped me reach out to millions. I had my own TV program through which I preached the Gospel. I even met the preacher who shared the Gospel when I was watching satellite TV in Iran that fateful day. I was so grateful to him, his ministry, and the opportunity to have worked with him. Who could've imagined that in a matter of a few years, I would be face-to-face with the person who introduced me to the Gospel almost 9,000 miles away?

After I enrolled in Bible school, I had to find another job that suited my schedule. Sometimes I worked at a youth facility from 11:00 PM to 7:00 AM, and went to class in the morning. I would share my love for Jesus with the young men there. One night, standing outside of the building was this fellow with whom I struck up a conversation. He angrily said he was AWOL. When I shared that Jesus died for him, he said he had tried Jesus before. But after hearing my testimony and urging, he decided to give Jesus another chance. For whatever reason that young man's face was red with rage, but when I laid my hands on him and prayed, a supernatural peace came upon him. I asked if he would like to give his heart to Jesus. He agreed and I guided him through the prayer of salvation. I gave him a pocket-size New Testament, which he immediately began reading. How awesome it is to share the love of Jesus with people who are broken, and to see salvation happen in a moment!

It's unfortunate that a politically correct culture has been created in the West, and people have been cowered into not sharing the Gospel of Jesus Christ so as not to offend certain groups. Even in some public places, we cannot openly express our faith in Jesus. The mere mention of His name incites unpleasant encounters. They call it "separation of Church and state," but this law was designed to protect the Church and Christians from government control of people's faith practices. Why is there such strong resistance against a group of people whose contributions to society, schools, orphanages, and hospitals, to name a few – are a clear manifestation of God's grace and goodness? As Christians, we must be free to do great things, especially share the Word of Life.

I'm so grateful to the Lord for bringing me to the United States. I love this country and it's my home now. I know our citizenship is in heaven, but it is wonderful to be well-ordered and clean in America! There is no place on earth I'd rather be. This Godly nation has been a refuge to millions of people who were unwanted in their home countries merely because of their faith, or who sought a better life and future. People who bash America, especially millennials whose collective "globalist" thinking has been influenced by liberal college professors, have no clue what they are saying. We must pray for our nation and bless it. America has been the land of opportunity, second chances and new beginnings for many people who were treated poorly in their own countries.

In Iran, the Islamic regime taught us to burn the American flag, but I have honored this flag since becoming a Christian. Indeed, it's a symbol of the countless men and women who have sacrificed their lives, so you and I could enjoy many freedoms in this country. God bless America and keep her for His glory.

In all the years I've been here, no one has ever treated me differently because of my race or skin color. Fortunately, I have been welcomed and accepted as a part of America since day one. I've had the privilege of meeting some of the kindest and most generous people since stepping into this country. It was America that God used to defeat Nazi Germany,

Imperialist Japan and Fascist Italy. It was America who reassured Russia to break the Berlin wall that separated families for years. It was America that saved Afghanistan from Soviet Union's takeover. Although we don't like wars but we live in a fallen world where there are so many bad people who want to dominate the world and America has been stopping them all over the world.

People who bash America either have been misinformed or are the very people who see America as a blockage to their world's domination. I was refreshed by hearing the story of a Holocaust survivor who gave a million dollar to the wounded American veterans in appreciation for his liberation on the D.Day.

When all hope had been lost suddenly the American troops rushed the shores of Normandy beach and rescuing millions of people in Europe. These are his own words as reported by Fox News on November 25th 2017:

"At 83 years old, I am one of the few remaining Holocaust survivors – thanks to the American troops who rescued me in what seems like a lifetime ago. Since World War II, I've felt a deep connection to American troops for saving my life – a feeling that resurfaces every year on Veterans Day and throughout the holiday giving season. And so this year I'm saying "thank you" to the American soldiers of the 1940s by donating $1 million to organizations serving wounded American veterans today.

My donation to the Wounded Warrior Project and the Services for Armed Forces program of the American Red Cross is my way of giving back, thanking previous generations of warriors for helping me. I hope this inspires others to give back as well. Even though more than 70 years have passed since my rescue, it's not too late to give back. That's a lesson I hope the next generation recognizes, because it's all too easy to let procrastination give way to inaction. But action is what brings hope to those who need it.

I have met many American people who I am lucky enough to call my friends. First, Americans saved us. Then decades later, they welcomed us.

As a child, I spent most of World War II hiding from Nazi invaders in my native France, where my parents moved after fleeing the pogroms in Poland. Unfortunately, with the German invasion in 1940, we were again at risk. On July 16, 1942, the French police led a big roundup of Jews in Paris. More than 13,000 Jews were detained before being deported to Nazi death camps.

The police came to our apartment at 6 a.m. My parents managed to take me to my aunt's home. She was married to a French soldier and was protected.

A few hours later, my mother was arrested as she and my brother were trying to get information about my father, who was hiding in a nearby grocery store. A concierge had pointed them out to the police. They ran, but my mother was not fast enough. She was detained and sent to the Auschwitz concentration camp. She perished there – probably within three weeks.

I was 7, and for the next two years I lived on borrowed time, shielded by other families on the outskirts of Paris. The same was true for my future wife, who was also a child in hiding. If the war had continued much longer, we would not have survived.

I vividly remember the arrival of the hundreds of thousands of American troops who landed in Normandy to liberate us in June 1944. They were our saviors, doling out packets of sweets to half-starved, war-weary children who had almost given up hope for freedom.

The gratitude I feel to these men is beyond words. They freed our country and they saved our lives. Without American troops, my family and I simply would not have existed. I think of that every time I look at our family photos.

Since the end of the war, life has been good to me. I've had a successful career as co-owner of one of Europe's largest home appliance retailers, working alongside my brothers. I've also enjoyed raising my family, celebrating extended family gatherings of 20 people.

My wife and I have a deep sense of gratitude for America. So in the early 1990s, freshly retired, we bought a home in South Florida. I travel with my wife each winter from our home in Paris to the warmth of Miami Beach. We still appreciate our second home there, where we now spend almost a third of our time.

I have met many American people who I am lucky enough to call my friends. First, Americans saved us. Then decades later, they welcomed us.

But as I watched news stories this fall of hurricanes, flooding and wildfires striking America, inflicting suffering among civilians and veterans alike, I realized that I still had an important task left to complete in my life. I had not yet given back to the American soldiers who saved my life nearly three-quarters of a century ago.

That is why I want to help modern American veterans today. They pursue the tradition of the young men who landed on the shores of Normandy in June 1944 and who I will never forget. In giving this donation, I want to thank Americans with all my heart for coming to rescue us in our hour of need.

But I also want to make a public stand in support of America. I hope that my donation can trigger a movement and lead others to take action. My story shows it's never too late to give back, especially for a cause that's close to your heart. If it wasn't too late for this octogenarian, it's not too late for you."

When I first came to the U.S., I noticed how people greeted and smiled at each other. This was strange to me because in Islamic or non-Christian nations, you don't see this kind of behavior. People here are mindful of cleanliness in their surroundings and don't throw trash on the streets. Driving in Oklahoma years ago, sometimes I would be distracted in traffic and not realize the light had turned green. The cars behind me never honked their horns and patiently waited for me to move. This happened to me many times. It might not be a big deal, but to me it's an expression of love, tolerance and forgiveness.

After I graduated from Rhema, the Holy Spirit led me to Los Angeles, California, where I helped a brother in Christ start two churches. Four years later, the Lord led me to start another church, of which I'm the pastor to this day. All our members are converts from Islam, except two Persian Jews who accepted the Messiah as their Savior.

I remember the first time I had the honor of meeting Pastor T.L. Osborn, one of the greatest evangelists of the 20th century and a humble man of God. When I heard that he was going to speak at a mega-church in Tulsa, Oklahoma, I didn't hesitate to go. After his amazing speech, I went to shake his hand, as did hundreds of other people. The crowd was thronging around him. I was right behind him and he suddenly turned around, pointed at me, and said, **"You will help us rebuild this country."** I looked around as I couldn't believe he was talking to me. I thought about it later and realized that God had brought me to America not to just chase and live the American Dream, but more importantly, to testify to the Lord's goodness, preach the truth of the Gospel, and lead the youth to Christ. I believe the best gift we can give people is to introduce them to Jesus. The Bible says in Psalm 33:12: *"Blessed is the nation whose God is the Lord."*

My church ministry is currently in Southern California. We have a studio where we produce Gospel messages to reach out to Persians, Americans and many other nations watch our teachings and preachings.. I travel domestically and overseas to share my testimony and the glorious Gospel of our Lord and Savior, Jesus Christ. I pray that I will be able to keep the faith and run with endurance the race that God has set before me. Please keep me in your prayers so that I'm able to finish my curse with Joy to be able to utter Paul's words who said:

"I have fought the good fight, I have finished the race, I have kept the faith. Finally, there is laid up for me the crown of righteousness, which the Lord, the righteous Judge, will give to me on that Day, and not to me only but also to all who have loved His appearing." I Timothy 4:7-8.

Chapter Seven

THE GLORY OF ANCIENT PERSIA

I visited Israel in 2015, and one day, after a condensed and exciting group tour, I left the hotel where I was staying to explore the beautiful city. It was Jerusalem Day and the streets were brimming with laughter and celebration. People of all ages waved their blue and white flags in the air, and locked arms in song and dance. I fortuitously came across a street called, you guessed it..."Cyrus". When I saw that, I was deeply moved that the Jewish people greatly respected a gentile who helped them 2,500 years ago. Cyrus is known as the Father of Persia just as George Washington is known as the Father of America.

Growing up, I was always fascinated by the history of great nations, but the Islamic system did everything in its power to bury the past, shrouding Iran's ancient glories in mystery and preventing the people from learning and connecting with their identity. I myself didn't know much about Iran's history until I got saved and began to read the Bible. Specifically, working on this book has brought to light the pivotal role of Persians in Biblical events. For example, I was amazed to learn in Ezra 7 that the Persian king wrote with his own hand and commissioned Ezra to go and teach the Law of Moses to the Jews and rebuild God's temple. Persians are awed when I tell them about these historical events. Somehow, tracing their roots kindles in them a sense of pride and a desire to walk in the footsteps of their ancestors.

It wasn't until I came to America that I gained access to a plethora of study resources. I also realized that most people's knowledge about Iran's history is superficial. I weeded through various historical accounts, some of which were biased and inaccurately told from different political vantage points. I spoke with experts who have devoted a good part of their lives to the study of Iran's history.

Along the way I learned about the inextricable link between the Persians and the Jewish people as described in the Bible. This is especially significant in light of the thousands of Iranian Muslims who have come to Christ in recent years. I see this as evidence of an underlying thread and of God's hand upon Iran over millennia. Christianity is currently the fastest growing religion in Iran despite heavy persecution by Islamic groups.

What's told in the next several pages is not an exhaustive account of Persian history, but instead a primer, a crash course if you will, that highlights some of the most significant events. One might wonder why I would even bother writing about antiquity. At some point during my studies, it became clear to me that events in Iran's ancient past, particularly the pounding Islamic invasions that had taken place even centuries before I was born, and the resurgence of Islam in Iran during my youth, have impacted my life's trajectory in ways that I would not comprehend until several years ago. For this reason, I felt that touching on history was vital to unpacking my own story.

If nothing else, I hope the brief account I share here sparks in you a genuine curiosity to dig deeper and investigate the beginnings and the development of one of history's greatest civilizations. It also bears repeating that not even the Persian Empire's indomitable might could withstand Islam's relentless assaults over the centuries, causing the Empire's eventual collapse. A seemingly innocuous ideology caused a supremely formidable and prosperous nation's descent into ashes, and holds it captive to this day. The West would be wise to call out and fight against the clear and present dangers posed by Islam. No nation is impervious to Islam's attacks, not even America.

ACHAEMENES EMPIRE

In 700 BC, there were many different tribes in Persia, until they all became united under one legendary figure named Achaemenes, who founded a dynasty. Persia emerged out of nothing, a rugged hostile terrain built only with invention and determination. The Persians traveled long distances in search of water until a Persian geologist and engineer built the first cornerstone of the Persian Empire, a breakthrough system of underground irrigation canals called Qanat. They began by harnessing gravity to exploit the natural topography of the land, allowing them to access the underground water that flowed from Alborz Mountain toward the Persian Gulf. Once they were able to bring the water to the surface and then channel massive amounts of water over long distances to the settlements and crops, these tribes were able to grow and flourish.

CYRUS THE GREAT

Cyrus the Great rose to power in 559 BC and this dynasty thrived. The Prophet Isaiah miraculously foretold the coming of Cyrus 140 years before his birth. He explained what Cyrus would do for the Jews before even he existed. The Babylonian ambassador to Persia, the Prophet Daniel, may have shown Cyrus what Isaiah had written about him.

At first, Cyrus did not know the God of Israel, but as evidenced in the book of Ezra (Chapter 1 verse 3), he later called the God of Israel the God of heaven. The Bible says the same thing in 2 Chronicles 36:22-23. What Cyrus did for the Jews was a shadow type of what Jesus has done for us. Cyrus set people free from Babylonian captivity, but Jesus sets us free from our sinful nature, from darkness, death, and hell.

By 554 BC, Cyrus had defeated all the local rivals and had become the undisputed ruler of Persia. He is one of the few that deserve to be called great for he rose to power, created and maintained one of the largest empires the world has ever seen. He was a political and economic genius with engineering and military savvy. King Cyrus is the most favored and respected king in Persian history and is highly esteemed among the Persians. Historians call him a humanist because he was a benevolent manager of men. The Jews also highly admired Cyrus and called him an anointed one.

Unlike many other conquerors and rulers who would plunder and destroy the territories of their conquest, Cyrus was a humble and righteous man who was gracious and merciful to the people he conquered. He respected their culture, religion and traditions. Among them were the Ionian Greeks who called him a just, worthy lawgiver and ruler. Only by the grace of God could a man in such power have a moral and just attitude toward others. Isaiah said of Cyrus:

Isaiah 45:13 *"I have raised him up in My righteousness: I will direct all his ways; He shall build My city and let My exiles go free, not for price nor reward," says the Lord of Hosts.*

The God of the Bible chose and commissioned King Cyrus to have a role in setting the Jews free from Babylonian captivity, so they could return to Jerusalem and rebuild the temple and the city, as told by the Prophet Isaiah:

Isaiah 44:28-Chapter 45:1, *It is I who says of Cyrus, "He is My shepherd! And He shall perform all My pleasure, saying to Jerusalem, You shall be built and to the temple, Your foundation shall be laid." Thus says the Lord to His anointed to Cyrus whose right hand I have held- to subdue nations before him and loose the armor of kings; to open before him the double doors so that the gates will not be shut.*

Cyrus's greatness was linked to God's call for his life. As we read in the Bible, Cyrus later acknowledged the God of Israel to whom he gave the credit for his success.

CYRUS'S CYLINDER

There is the famous Cyrus's Cylinder, which is currently in the possession of the British Museum. The text is written in Akkadian cuneiform script in the name of Persia's Achaemenid king, Cyrus the Great. It's engraved in a cylinder-shaped object and dates back to 6ᵗʰ century BC. Biblical scholars have considered the Cylinder's text as corroborative evidence of Cyrus's policy of the repatriation of the Jewish people following their Babylonian captivity, just as the Lord had commanded him. Cyrus attributed this mission to the LORD God of Israel as he said in the book of Ezra 1:1-4.

"Now in the first year of Cyrus king of Persia, that the word of the Lord by the mouth of Jeremiah might be fulfilled, the Lord stirred up the spirit of Cyrus king of Persia, so that he made a proclamation throughout all his kingdom, and also put it in writing, saying,

Thus says Cyrus king of Persia:

All the kingdoms of the earth the Lord God of heaven has given me. And He has commanded me to build Him a house at Jerusalem which is in Judah. 3 Who is among you of all His people? May his God be with him, and let him go up to Jerusalem which is in Judah, and build the house of the Lord God of Israel (He is God), which is in Jerusalem. 4 And whoever is left in any place where he dwells, let the men of his place help him with silver and gold, with goods and livestock, besides the freewill offerings for the house of God which is in Jerusalem."

Not only that, but Cyrus had also given the Jews all of the instruments of the temple which were taken by Nebuchadnezzar king of Babylon, as described in Ezra 1:7-11

King Cyrus also brought out the articles of the house of the Lord, which Nebuchadnezzar had taken from Jerusalem and put in the temple of his gods; 8 and Cyrus king of Persia brought them out by the hand of Mithredath the treasurer, and counted them out to Sheshbazzar the prince of Judah. 9 This is the number of them: thirty gold platters, one thousand silver platters, twenty-nine knives, 10 thirty gold basins, four hundred and ten silver basins of a similar kind, and one thousand other articles. 11 All the articles of gold and silver were five thousand four hundred. All these Sheshbazzar took with the captives who were brought from Babylon to Jerusalem.

The inscription on Cyrus' tomb reads: "O man, whoever thou art, from wheresoever thou cometh, for I know you shall come, I am Cyrus, who founded the Persian Empire.

Grudge me not, therefore, this little earth that covers my body." Cyrus the Great.

CONSTRUCTION OF PASARGADAE

Cyrus was an innovative builder and his standards were particularly high. His building projects were reflective of his conquests. Persians also borrowed the best, most advanced and sophisticated ideas of engineering methods from the cultures they conquered, then they developed them even further to technologies uniquely their own. In 550 BC, Cyrus launched one of the most ambitious engineering projects anywhere in the ancient world, the Persian Empire's great first capital city at Pasargadae. King Cyrus's tomb is currently located at Pasargadae and it's intact.

CONSTRUCTION OF PERSEPOLIS- DARIUS I

Another enormous building project was the construction of Persepolis under king Darius. This was the second but largest ceremonial capital city of the Persian Empire. It's situated 60 km northeast of the city of Shiraz in Fars Province, Iran, only two hours away from where I was born and one hour away from where I was raised. I have visited the majestic remains of Persepolis, the earliest of which date back to 515 BC. It exemplifies the Achaemenid style of architecture. UNESCO declared the ruins of Persepolis a World Heritage Site in 1979.

As the Persian Empire was expanding, building projects also started. Stone workers, wood workers, painters, brick makers, architects, artisans, and laborers along with tons of materials were brought in from far reaches of empire. But unlike other empires who forced people into hard labor without wage, Darius, like Cyrus, paid wages to the people who were working and building Persepolis. They refused to enslave their new subjects, which was uncommon among most ancient empires built by massive armies of slave labor. Women were involved and brought their respective talents into buildings and designs, and they were paid accordingly. Some walls were as tall as 60 ft. high and 35 ft. thick. Persepolis was adorned with gold, silver, expensive tapestry, and colorful tiles. The walls were carved with the depictions of visiting dignitaries from conquered lands who brought their peace offering to the king and pledged their loyalty to the empire. Persepolis' spectacular engineering achievements extended far beyond the city walls. Its intricately designed and constructed water and drainage system was unparalleled anywhere at the time. They were able to direct water from the Qanat system. No expense was spared since Persepolis would be the signature monument of Persian powers and glory.

Even during his most ambitious local infrastructure projects, Darius never stopped expanding his empire, which grew to a staggering size that included modern Iran, Pakistan, Parts of Afghanistan, Armenia, Turkey,

Syria, Egypt, Lebanon, Jordan, Israel, parts of central Asia all the way to northern India.

POSTAL SYSTEM

Darius started two amazing building projects to connect the farthest parts of the empire: a road that would stretch 1,500 miles of the Persian Empire and the other connected the Red Sea to the Mediterranean. In 515 BC, his engineers built a massive stone highway, one that connected North Africa to India, a 1,500-mile long highway called the Royal Road, linked by 1,100 rest stations and inns every 18 miles. This was also the beginning of a postal system by which letters were delivered to the farthest parts of the empire.

DARIUS CANAL

Darius wanted to connect the vast riches of North Africa, so he built a gateway. His engineers devised a giant east-west 130-mile long canal linking the Mediterranean and the Red Sea. With the Persian knowledge of hydrology, Darius's engineers used digging tools to first open the canal, and then clear any sand and line it with stone, making it ready for the ships to sail. The canal took seven years to build. The massive labor force consisted of Egyptian stonecutters and canal builders. Finally, the Red Sea was connected with the Nile River for trade.

PERSIA VS. GREECE

By 500 BC, the Persian Empire was the largest empire the world had ever seen, even exceeding the wealth and size of the Roman Empire at its height four centuries later. At 494 BC, Darius put down revolts in some cities in the coast of Turkey. These revolts were supported by Athens, so Darius wanted to teach Athens a lesson. He wanted to march on Greece and attack Athens, but there was a problem. The Aegean Sea was between

Asia Minor and Greece. Darius brilliantly used a large number of boats to create a bridge by lining them up next to each other and stabilized them by connecting them through ropes and rods. This successful idea helped 70,000 Persian troops cross the sea into Greece at its narrowest point, the Bosphorus. Thus, Asia was connected to Europe.

BATTLE OF MARATHON

In late August, year 490 BC, Darius's army had successfully marched into Greece and taken Macedonia. Now his Army was destined to meet the Greek general and politician Themistocles and an army from Athens at the famous battle of Marathon. The Persians mowed down the Greek army in a clash where the Greeks were outnumbered by ten to one. A reduced Greek force faced the Persian army head-on and the Persians had an easy victory. The remaining Greek force had split into two, opening two other fronts against the Persians. It turned into two bloody slaughter pits. The Persians suffered heavy losses and retreated. For the Greeks, it was a major victory but for the Persians, just a speed bump on their path to world domination. Phidippides, the one who acted as courier, ran 26 miles the same day and brought the news of victory from Marathon and addressed the magistrates in session in Athens. That's where we get the word Marathon. The Greeks in Athens were anxious how the battle had ended. "Joy to you, we've won" he said, and there and then he died, breathing his last breath with the words "Joy to you". – Lucian translated by K. Kilburn.

While preparing a second attack against Greece in 486 BC, Darius died on his way to put down a rebellion in Egypt. Leaving behind a legacy and an empire that we define as the notion of power and glory, his body was embalmed and entombed in the rock-cut sepulcher in the heart of a mountain at Naqsh-e Rustam, located about seven miles northwest of Persepolis, in Fars Province, Iran. I visited this amazing site. The rock-cut tomb was carved in the shape of a cross. This location houses a few of the Persian monarchs.

KING XERXES

Darius named his son Xerxes as his successor. Xerxes became king after his father died. He had to first put down some rebellion in Egypt and Babylon that his father never got a chance to do. Then ten years after his father retreated from Greece, he went after the Greeks. Perhaps he wanted to finish what his father started, but some historians believe that Xerxes was making a preemptive strike. Defeated at Marathon, the Persians no longer intimidated the Greeks who were emerging as a major power and a rival. A coalition of profoundly different city-state, from democracies to dictatorships, they were united only by one creed, their hatred of Persia. The ancient world was on the verge of a second Persian War. The outcome would set up the foundation for the modern world. Xerxes used almost the same strategy by building a bridge and moved the Persian troops into Europe. So for a short moment, Europe and Asia were connected.

Xerxes wanted to overwhelm the Greeks by superior numbers both at sea and land. But general Themistocles, the same person who helped fight the Persians in the first war at Marathon, knew that the Greeks couldn't defeat the Persians on land, so they focused their campaign on defeating the Persians at sea in order to destroy their navy. He was the king whose wife was Queen Vashti (as we read in the Bible's Book of Esther). Queen Vashti was dethroned after she refused to attend the state dinner where war with Greece would be decided. In August 480 BC, the two armies met at a place chosen by the Greeks, Thermopylae, a narrow path that only one chariot at a time could pass. For days, the massive Persian army was stalled, backed up at the wrong side of the path, just as Greeks had planned. In the meantime, Themistocles left with most of his army without Persians realizing it, leaving only a token force of 6,000 Spartans behind. Like his father, Xerxes was about to head into a Greek trap. When they finally broke through the narrow path, the Persians easily destroyed the force Themistocles had left behind.

Xerxes marched toward Athens, but when he reached the city, Athens was deserted. Xerxes thought he was deceived and wanted to make Greeks pay for it. For generations, tolerance for their conquests had been the hallmark of Persian kings, but not this time. In a very un-Persian like act, he burned Athens to the ground. Xerxes regretted it immediately and the following morning, he ordered Athens rebuilt. But it was too late. The deed was done. But this war was far from over. At the same time, Themistocles was setting up his trap that would lure the massive Persian navy at the narrow bay of Salamis. Then he unleashed a surprise attack. Using their powerful battleships, the Greeks attacked and destroyed the Persian navy at sea. It was a decisive victory for the Greeks. Xerxes returned home defeated. The Persian Wars launched Athens into its Golden Age, but left the Persian Empire vulnerable. Esther became Queen after Xerxes' wife Vashti refused to attend one of the king's feasts. The king became furious and dethroned her. Later Esther found favor in his sight and she became Queen.

In 465 BC, King Xerxes was assassinated. His killer was Artabanus the Hyrcanian, a Persian political figure during the Achaemenid Dynasty who was Regent of Persia for a few months. Xerxes was buried with his father and his tomb is still in modern day Iran. Xerxes left the empire to his son, Artaxerxses.

PURIM

The Jews in Persia were exiles that Cyrus liberated from captivity when he conquered Babylon. During Xerxes's time, a man who held a lot of power in the country, Haman, plotted to kill the Jews. When Mordecai learned about the plot, he urged Queen Esther to use her influence to thwart it. As a result, the Jews on the verge of extermination were saved, and their enemies, including Haman and his sons, were executed and destroyed. To this day, Jews celebrate this enormous victory, it's called Purim. Here is the Biblical account of the story according to Esther 9:18-28.

"But the Jews who were at Shushan assembled together on the thirteenth day, as well as on the fourteenth; and on the fifteenth of the month they rested, and made it a day of feasting and gladness. Therefore the Jews of the villages who dwelt in the unwalled towns celebrated the fourteenth day of the month of Adar with gladness and feasting, as a holiday, and for sending presents to one another.

And Mordecai wrote these things and sent letters to all the Jews, near and far, who were in all the provinces of King Ahasuerus (Xerxes), to establish among them that they should celebrate yearly the fourteenth and fifteenth days of the month of Adar, as the days on which the Jews had rest from their enemies, as the month which was turned from sorrow to joy for them, and from mourning to a holiday; that they should make them days of feasting and joy, of sending presents to one another and gifts to the poor. So the Jews accepted the custom which they had begun, as Mordecai had written to them, because Haman, the son of Hammedatha the Agagite, the enemy of all the Jews, had plotted against the Jews to annihilate them, and had cast Pur (that is, the lot), to consume them and destroy them; but when Esther[c] came before the king, he commanded by letter that this[d] wicked plot which Haman had devised against the Jews should return on his own head, and that he and his sons should be hanged on the gallows.

So they called these days Purim, after the name Pur. Therefore, because of all the words of this letter, what they had seen concerning this matter, and what had happened to them, the Jews established and imposed it upon themselves and their descendants and all who would join them, that without fail they should celebrate these two days every year, according to the written instructions and according to the prescribed time, that these days should be remembered and kept throughout every generation, every family, every province, and every city, that these days of Purim should not fail to be observed among the Jews, and that the memory of them should not perish among their descendants."

Haman was not Persian originally; he was a descendant of Agag, the king of the Amalekites, a people who were wiped out in certain areas by King Saul and David. It seems that the hatred for the Jews has been a historical and perpetual factor. I believe it's because they were the people who carried the promise of the Messiah whom the devil tried to destroy.

KING ARTAXERXES

King Artaxerxes was determined to take Persia back to its golden days. He began to complete the construction of Persepolis, which was started forty years before by his grandfather, Darius the Great. He oversaw the construction of one of the greatest engineering projects known as the "hall of a hundred columns." The columns built in this hall were 100 ft. tall and very precise using a remarkable lift technology. The architecture and the vastness of the hall and the jungle of columns amazed any foreign dignitary who visited Persepolis.

By the 4th century BC, Persian engineering was still the finest in the world. But as soaring columns and shining places were improving, the empire's enemies were planning to go to war with Persia. When Athens supported a rebellion in Egypt, and Greeks occupied the capital city of Memphis, Artaxerxes left Persepolis and his building projects. He launched a military campaign to kick the Greeks out of Memphis and bring Egypt back under the control of Persia. This was a successful battle for the Persians.

NEHEMIAH

As I said before, during the busy days of conquest and building projects, God was working on His own primary plan to preserve, protect, and restore the Jews to Judea. God's purpose was to bring the Messiah into the world, who would conquer our hearts and establish His heavenly and righteous Kingdom.

A Jewish man by the name of Nehemiah was King Artaxerxes cup-bearer, a very sensitive and trustworthy position for the King's life was in his hands. His job was to make sure that the food and drink that Artaxerxes consumed were not poisoned. I believe that just like Esther, Nehemiah was placed in that position by the Lord to further His plan of rebuilding the walls of Jerusalem.

Although Cyrus the Great freed the Jews and commissioned them to go to Jerusalem and rebuild the temple, just as the Lord had moved his spirit, the Jews in Judea had not completely rebuilt the city yet. Due to much persecution and opposition of the local enemies, they had become disinterested and discouraged. After Nehemiah's brother along with some other Jewish men came from Jerusalem, they reported to Nehemiah the circumstances of the Jewish people. The walls of Jerusalem were broken, and the Jews were mocked by their neighbors. Nehemiah was grieved. As his job required, he couldn't appear before the king with a saddened face. But after three months of fasting and prayer, he finally shared the reason for his grief with the king and the Lord graciously gave him favor with Artaxerxes. He was given permission, resources, and other necessary tools to go back and rebuild Jerusalem. Israel was a part of the Persian Empire at the time.

Nehemiah departed the comfortable life in the palace to go work with rubble, dirt, stones, and a group of oppressed and discouraged people, and of course, he had to face the hostile enemies. It's interesting what Scripture says about how God always uses the lowly things of the world to confound the wise and mighty. In the great Persian Empire with its magnificent art and engineering, nobody gave much importance to Jerusalem and the Jews, but they were the most important part of God's plan. Similarly, while the Roman Empire was building and expanding, and Herod was developing his region, the baby Jesus was born in a stable in Bethlehem. That baby was God's Son and the savior of humanity. God uses ordinary people to do great and mighty things.

Earlier in 458 BC, Artaxerxes sent a group of Jews to Jerusalem under the leadership of Ezra. With resources and valuables to enhance the temple for worship, Ezra's responsibility was to revive people spiritually and stir their hearts and morals for the things of the Lord, to teach the Law of Moses, and bring people back to God. The Jews were opposed and accused of wanting to rebel against the king. Thus, many times the work of rebuilding of the temple was stopped. But these efforts didn't stop Ezra and Nehemiah.

ALEXANDER THE GREAT

In 424 BC, Artaxerxes died and left a power vacuum. For eight solid decades of infighting and neglect, the Persian Empire was getting more vulnerable due to corruption. Meanwhile, a young Macedonian prince, Alexander, who was fascinated by Herodotus' accounts of Cyrus and the Persian Empire, set his eyes on conquering the world. Alexander admired the Persian kings and the Achaemenid Dynasty so much that he called himself the last Achaemenid king.

Alexander rose to power and began to prepare for war with Persia during the reign of Darius III. Within four years, they had many conflicts and fierce battles, and the Persians were slowly pushed back to their doorstep.

In 330 BC, Alexander was at the door of the crown jewel of the Persian Empire, the capital city of Persepolis. Alexander had adopted the Persian policy of respecting the defeated. None of his soldiers was allowed to plunder and pillage the lands they had conquered. But during the celebration of their victory, the treasury was pillaged and then one of the saddest acts of arson in history took place. Persepolis was burned to the ground. Some historians believe that the soldiers were drunk during the celebration and the fire may have been an accident. Others believe that it was a symbolic act or perhaps the Greeks avenged what Xerxes did when he burned Athens. Some believe that Alexander was remorseful after Persepolis was burned.

Darius III was captured and in the summer of 330 BC, he was murdered. The last Achaemenid king was dead. Alexander gave Darius III a magnificent funeral and later married his daughter. He would also chase down and kill the murderer of King Darius III. Alexander declared himself an Achaemenid Persian king. Thus, he added the last chapter to the story of an empire that expanded to three continents and endured for over 2,700 years.

Alexander didn't create an empire; instead, he conquered one. Cyrus the Great pioneered and built the empire that existed long before Alexander was born. The empire's legacy of culture, engineering, and luxury would be around long after Alexander's death in 323 BC.

Interestingly enough, the Lord showed the Greco-Persian Wars and the rise of the Roman Empire to the Prophet Daniel, a Jewish man who served as a minister to Babylonian and Persian Kings, long before these events occurred.

Here is the vision as told in Daniel 8:1-12:

"In the third year of the reign of King Belshazzar a vision appeared to me—to me, Daniel—after the one that appeared to me the first time. I saw in the vision, and it so happened while I was looking, that I was in Shushan, the citadel, which is in the province of Elam; and I saw in the vision that I was by the River Ulai. Then I lifted my eyes and saw, and there, standing beside the river, was a ram which had two horns, and the two horns were high; but one was higher than the other, and the higher one came up last. I saw the ram pushing westward, northward, and southward, so that no animal could withstand him; nor was there any that could deliver from his hand, but he did according to his will and became great.

And as I was considering, suddenly a male goat came from the west, across the surface of the whole earth, without touching the ground; and the goat had a notable horn between his eyes. Then he came to the ram that had two horns, which I had seen standing beside the river, and ran at him with furious power. And I saw him confronting the ram; he was moved with rage against him, attacked the ram, and broke his two horns. There was no power in the ram to withstand him, but he cast him down to the ground and trampled him; and there was no one that could deliver the ram from his hand.

Therefore the male goat grew very great; but when he became strong, the large horn was broken, and in place of it four notable ones came up toward the four winds of heaven. And out of one of them came a little horn which grew exceedingly great toward the south, toward the east, and toward the Glorious Land. And it grew up to the host of heaven; and it cast down some of the host and some of the stars to the ground, and trampled them. He even exalted himself as high as the Prince of the host; and by him the daily sacrifices were taken away, and the place of His sanctuary was cast down. Because of transgression, an army was given over to the horn to oppose the daily sacrifices; and he cast truth down to the ground. He did all this and prospered."

ISLAM IN PERSIA

The Persians indeed had power struggles and lost buildings, influence and land, but their culture and morals were preserved. They would move on and rebuild. However, when Islam came to Persia, it destroyed the morals, and replaced and reprogrammed the great, rich culture with imposed Islamic rules and rituals. Over time, the great ancient Persia turned into ashes and hasn't seen glory days ever since it was conquered by Islam in 7th century AD. Iran is now known as the first state sponsor of terrorism and the second violator of human rights in the world.

Cyrus, Darius, Xerxes, Artaxerxes were great men and strong conquerors, but no different from other men in that they, too, were conquered by the grave. These were instruments that God used in their own time to sustain Israel, so through them Messiah the Savior could come. **There is only one person who conquered the grave, the Lord Jesus Christ**. I believe one day we will see some of these monarchs in heaven since many of them accepted the Lord God of Israel, the only true God.

Although Persia was a powerful empire and they had their own agenda, it's clear that God was quietly advancing His plan. For the Jews, Persia was a safe haven where they flourished. Some even held high political offices that helped the Jews survive hostile enemies and rebuild Jerusalem. The Jews had to survive and return to Judea in order for God's plan of salvation to be fulfilled. These kings and their glories withered, but God gave the world a King that would reign in righteousness and win people over with love. His name is King Jesus, the King of kings and Lord of lords. This King laid down His life and was a servant to His followers.

Chapter Eight

ISLAM

"Islam is as dangerous in a man as rabies in a dog."
-Winston Churchill

The world recognizes Islam as one of the major "faiths", but there's so much more to this "religion" than meets the eye. Islam, which means "submission", is a judicial, political, and military system cloaked as a religion. Islam is not a race of people, but a belief system with the mission of building a theocracy of which Allah is the supreme ruler. A Trues as stipulated in their "holy" book, the Quran.

Before I further substantiate the above claim, I want to assure you that the purpose of this book isn't bigotry. This is neither hateful targeting of Islam to prove my point or unleash any bitterness toward Muslims, nor is it so-called "Islamophobia." Scrutinizing Islam is not attacking and maligning a group of people. Quite the opposite, I'm helping to expose an ideology steeped in a 1,400-year history of violence that continues to hold its followers captive and using them to harm others as well as themselves. I want to bring awareness about how harshly women are being treated under Islam. What I'm presenting to you is the naked truth about Islam. Please read on and make an informed judgment based on my own experience living under Islam's tyranny in Iran, and evidential sources such as the Quran, the Hadiths (Muhammad's sayings) and other Islamic textbooks.

The Quran teaches that all non-Muslims are enemies and infidels (kafirs) who are deluded from the truth. When Muslims see unbelievers holding positions of power in the world or dominating the economy, they judge these as abominations. Therefore, they fight for Islamic supremacy. Not only must Muslims be in charge, but unbelievers must be humiliated, subjugated, or killed.

The two main branches of Islam are Shia and Sunni. Shi'ites believe that Muhammad's successor was Ali ibn e Abitaleb, the first Shi'ite imam and Muhammad's son-in-law. The last of the twelve succeeding imams was Mahdi Al-Montazer who, according to Shi'ite Muslims, had disappeared, but will return to rule the world one day. He will come when the whole world is in chaos and destroy the unbelievers. The condition for his return is chaos, which Shi'ites purposely create to hasten his return of the last imam.

Sunnis, on the other hand, believe that Muhammad's successor was Abu Bakr, the first Caliph. They hold that the whole world should come under Islam to establish a worldwide Caliphate. Both groups use violence and call for the destruction of Israel and the eradication of the Jews.

Islam is absurdly obsessed with taking over the world. For centuries, its followers have been fighting to establish a worldwide caliphate. I challenge you to put any of the fifty-one Islamic nations around the world under a historical and social microscope, and study Islam's catastrophic impact on them. Previously, I gave you the example of Iran (ancient Persia). One of today's most serious problems worldwide is Islamic terrorism, which according to studies, kills more people globally than those killed by natural disasters. It's no less than an existential threat to the Western civilization and every non-Muslim nation.

MUHAMMAD AND THE BIRTH OF ISLAM

Muhammad was born in 570 AD in the Arabian city of Mecca. In 609 AD, he asserted that he was a prophet of "God." Specifically, he claimed that while in a desert, he entered a cave called Harrah and an "angel" appeared to him and gave him revelations. Oddly enough, this visitation terrified Muhammad so much and caused him to be suicidal. He would run to his wife Khadijah who comforted and covered him with a blanket. For a while, Muhammad didn't have a normal life. He wanted to hurl himself over a cliff and suffered from epileptic seizures, which were manifestations of demonic possession. At the urging of his wife, Muhammad eventually listened to the "angel" who gave him verbal instructions, which would make up the Quran.

The series of visitations began on December 22, 609 AD, when Muhammad was about forty years old, and continued until his death in 632 AD. Whatever Muhammad heard, he spoke, and since he was illiterate, he dictated the revelations to his followers who recorded them.

ALLAH

Muhammad preached about Allah whom he believed to be the "one true God." It's important to note that the name of Muhammad's father's was Abdullah, which means "servant of Allah." This was also the name of a Meccan idol that was bigger in size than others, for which reason they called it Allah, meaning "the one." Therefore, Muhammad wasn't teaching anything new, but preaching a god who was talking to him through the "angel".

An interesting fact about this big idol is that the tribes of that region considered the three sensuous statues of women at the entrance to Mecca to be Allah's daughters. Their names were al Uzza (star goddess), al Lat (sun goddess), and Manat (goddess of fate). It is true, as Muslims claim, that Allah had no son (as did Jehovah), but they forget to mention (or don't know) that he had three daughters. Because Muhammad didn't have many followers in Mecca, to get people's attention, he introduced Allah's daughters and encouraged his followers to worship them (Surah 53). However, Muhammad later denounced those revelations and said they were from Satan, indicating that he couldn't distinguish between revelations from God and those from Satan.

The famous book *"The Satanic Verses"* written by Sir Ahmed Salman Rushdie, the British-Indian writer referred to the satanic verses and Muhammad. He received many death threats. Ayatollah Khomeini the supreme leader of the Islamic regime in Iran issued a *"Fatwa"* calling for his assassination. The British government put put him under police protection.

People ask me whether Allah is the same God that Jews and Christians worship, to which my answer is unequivocally no. Allah is not the name for God in Arabic. Allah is a certain idol that Arabs used to worship. Notice in their motto or Shahada, they say, "There is no god but Allah," so if the name for God was Allah, then the word "God" must have been used twice in this motto. Just as Christians say, "There is no God but Jesus," God is the general name, but Jesus is the specific name of a person. Allah is not the same God as Yahweh or Jesus. In fact, Muslims believe that before Muhammad's time, Arabs worshiped idols and even buried their female babies, and they didn't know who God was. Allah was an idol known as a moon god. It had nothing to do with Christianity and Judaism.

The word for "God" in Arabic is "Elaha" It means a divine supreme being. In the Islamic motto reads: "There is no "Elaha" except "Allah" and Muhammad is his messenger." Allah is not "God".

After Islamic invasions, they were forced to learn and speak Arabic. Therefore, the minorities in Arab countries call God "Allah," which I believe is a mistake. The name for God in Arabic is Elaha or Rab, not Allah.

SURAHS: MECCA VS. MEDINA

The Quran consists of 114 chapters known as surahs that are classified as Meccan or Medinan. Islam was peaceful in the beginning, but after the people of Mecca rejected Muhammad's message, and even his own uncle disapproved of him, he moved to Medina.

The most prosperous people in Medina were Jews and Christians, while many native Arabs were poor. Muhammad capitalized on this economic disparity to incite violence among the Arabs by claiming that they were disenfranchised because Jews and Christians controlled everything and protected each other. Muhammad promised the Arabs they could change that. He gathered small gangs of people who hated the other groups for their success in business. (Hitler used a similar propaganda after World War I when he ranted and convinced many Germans that the Jews despised them and controlled everything. It's no different from the Palestinians of today who hold Israel responsible for their problems.)

Muhammad also promised his followers wealth and a fleshly paradise. After he had gathered enough followers, he and his militia attacked and robbed the caravans coming out of Mecca in retaliation for his rejection, which he called a judgment and punishment for unbelievers. Soon he was able to assemble an army of ten thousand. After Meccans saw what happened to their caravans, they sent an army with the next caravans. Muhammad came with his army and a war broke out, known as the Battle of Badr, and they prevailed, leading to more conquests, killings, and women and goods being taken as spoils of war.

While Meccan surahs are nonviolent. Medinan surahs are the opposite because Muhammad spoke according to his power. His violence increased in proportion to his power. According to Islam, Medinan surahs supersede the Meccan surahs. Therefore, the revelations that Muhammad received later are considered more reliable than the former ones. Muhammad constantly changed his position, not for the better but for worse. To understand the many contradictions in the Quran, one must first know where the surahs were revealed.

Muslims are diplomatic only when they are a minority but when they are a majority, they become violent, intolerant and aggressive. Muhammad was peaceful when he was in Mecca for twelve years (known as the "hardship period"), when he didn't have power. He said in the Quran:

> **Surah 2:256**
> "Let there be no compulsion in religion: Truth stands out clear from Error: whoever rejects evil and believes in Allah hath grasped the most trustworthy hand-hold, that never breaks. And Allah heareth and knoweth all things."

A good example of how some of today's Muslims adhere to the foregoing admonition by Muhammad is my friend Kenten's story. When he worked as a manager in Colorado, he began to hire Muslim Somali refugees for his employer. As this group's population within the company grew, the Somalis demanded five prayer breaks daily. During times of prayer, the entire company had to shut down the lines and operations, a disruption that the management calculated would result in millions of dollars in losses. The demands of the Somalis who came as poor refugees effectively changed the dynamics of the company. This is what happens when Muslims immigrate to Western countries and increase in numbers. Soon they will require Islamic holidays and dietary foods, etc.

Again, pre-Medina, Muhammad seemed "tolerant" of other religions:

> **Surah 2:62**
> "Those who believe (in the Qur'an), and those who follow the Jewish (scriptures), and the Christians and the Sabeans, any who believes in Allah and the Last

Day, and works righteousness, shall have their reward
with their Lord; on them shall be no fear, nor shall
they grieve."

However, when he moved to Medina and had a robust army of thousands,
he changed his mind and said the following about unbelievers, particularly
the Jews and the Christians.

Surah 9:29
"Fight (actual text in Arabic says kill) those who
believe not in Allah nor the Last Day, nor hold that
forbidden which hath been forbidden by Allah and
His Messenger, nor acknowledge the religion of
Truth (Islam), even if they are of the People of the
Book (Jews and Christians), until they pay the Jizya
(punishment by paying blood money) with willing
submission, and feel themselves subdued and
humiliated."

Surah 9:5
"But when the forbidden months are past, then fight
and slay the Pagans wherever ye find them, and
seize them, beleaguer them, and lie in wait for them
in every stratagem but if they repent, and establish
regular prayers and practice regular charity, then
open the way for them: for Allah is Oft-forgiving,
Most Merciful."

Surah 5:51
"O ye who believe! Take not the Jews and the
Christians for your friends and protectors: They
are but friends and protectors to each other. And he
amongst you that turns to them (for friendship) is of
them. Verily Allah guideth not a people unjust."

It is clear that Muslims cannot be in friendship with Christians and Jews, and at the same time follow Islam. Some Muslim scholars try to justify Surah 5:51 by saying it only pertains to a certain group of Christians and Jews. However, Muhammad cursed Christians for believing Jesus is the Son of God. All Christians, then and now, believe Jesus is the Son of God who was crucified for the remission of our sins. This is one of the most fundamental aspects of the Christian faith, but Islamic text addresses the issue of Jesus' divinity as follows:

> **Surah 4:157**
> **"That they said (in boast), 'We killed Christ Jesus the son of Mary, the Messenger of Allah.;- but they killed him not, nor crucified him, but so it was made to appear to them, and those who differ therein are full of doubts, with no (certain) knowledge, but only conjecture to follow, for of a surety they killed him not..."**

Even to this day, some Muslims use the peaceful Meccan verses to show the West that Islam teaches peace, equality and justice, but the moment they have power they shift gears and wield the Medinan verses to violently subdue and control communities and nations.

MUHAMMAD'S DEEDS

Unlike what some people want you to believe, Muhammad was not a peaceful man at all. Early Muslim records are filled with acts of extreme brutality carried out by Muhammad and his followers - executions, assassinations, beheadings, and torture. There were forty-seven wars in the history of Islam, and in twenty-two of them, Muhammad himself drew the sword. Additionally, after Muslims conquered a city, they raped women who were to be sold as slaves, even as they grieved for their dead husbands, fathers and sons. Even today, we know that followers of Muhammad are committing the same heinous acts.

Muhammad subdued all freedoms and ordered his followers to assassinate people for writing poetry against Islam. He also mandated the violent deaths of those who insulted him. What now follow are some examples of Muhammad's horrific acts.

Kaab Ben Ashraf was a Jew who never physically attacked Muhammad or his followers, but he did write some harsh poetry. Muhammad commanded his followers to kill him. They sliced him from his stomach to his groin over the poetry he wrote.

Likewise, Abu 'Afak, also Jewish, was over a hundred years old. He was a staunch political opponent of Muhammad and wrote poetry criticizing Muslims. Muhammad asked, "Who will deal with this rascal for me?" Salim, one of Muhammad's followers, obliged, and stabbed Abu 'Afak in the liver while he was asleep, killing him.

Then when a woman by the name of Asmah heard that Muhammad and his followers killed an old man over poetry, she, too, wrote a poem about their crime and she called the people around to stand up to Muhammad. When he heard this, he asked, "Who will deal with Asmah for me?" A devotee of Muhammad then went into a room where Asmah was breastfeeding one of her five children, and stabbed her to death.

Another man was heard saying he would never accept Islam, so Muhammad's follower took a bow and shot an arrow through the man's eye socket, which came out the back of his head. Muhammad blessed that follower for his dedication, and ordered the death of a slave girl who wrote a song that made fun of Muhammad.

Another man was executed and a woman named Sarah was trampled to death by a horse, as both spoke against and insulted Muhammad. One day after a battle, Muhammad commanded his followers to torture Kannana, a man who hid money that the Muslims were after. They lit a fire on Kannana's chest which made him confess, but they still cut off his head.

According to Surah 4:3 in the Quran, Muslim men may marry up to four women, but Surah 33:50 allows only Muhammad to have as many wives as he wanted. This self-proclaimed prophet from "God" had revelations that permitted him to have more sexual partners than others. Muhammad's marriage to six-year-old Ayisha was consummated when she was nine and he was fifty-three. Today we call this pedophilia and abhorrent child abuse. I want to pose this question to Muslims: **What kind of "prophet" are you following?**

The above are just some examples set by Muhammad, and we know that even today many Muslims practice the same things around the world. In countries like Afghanistan, Saudi Arabia, Lebanon, Syria, Iraq, etc., child marriages are encouraged because it was the Sunnah (the way of life) of the prophet Muhammad. Many adult Muslim men have married children who are many years, even decades, younger than they are.

The Quran is not God's word, Muhammad is not His messenger, and Allah is not God.

Islam will never be a friend to the West and the Western culture or the Western values and Israel. Islam perceives the Westerners as infidels. Some Muslim countries may be a superficial ally of the West and America for their own advantage o to get financial and military support but in reality, the Islamists hate America and the West. Pakistan has been receiving Billions of dollars in aid from the United States but they are harbouring the terrorists and has become a safe haven for the Jihadist and Taliban. Bin Laden was living safely in Pakistan until US government found out and even when the marines raided his house, Pakistanis were not happy. They burn the US flag and don't like the West.

TIMELINE OF MUHAMMAD'S LIFE (A.D)

570 - Born in Mecca

576 - Orphaned upon death of mother

595 - Marries Kadijah - older, wealthy widow

610 - Reports first revelations at age of 40

619 - Protector uncle dies

622 - Emigrates from Mecca to Medina (the Hijra)

623 - Orders raids on Meccan caravans

624 - Battle of Badr (victory)

624 - Evicts Qaynuqa Jews from Medina

624 - Orders assassination of Abu Afak

624 - Orders assassination of Asma bint Marwan

624 - Orders the assassination of Ka'b al-Ashraf

625 - Battle of Uhud (defeat)

625 - Evicts Nadir Jews

627 - Battle of the Trench (victory)

627 - Massacre of the Qurayza Jews

628 - Signing of the Treaty of Hudaibiya with Mecca

628 - Destruction and subjugation of the Khaybar Jews

629 - Orders first raid into Christian lands at Muta (defeat)

630 - Conquers Mecca by surprise (along with other tribes)

631 - Leads second raid into Christian territory at Tabuk (no battle)

632 - Dies

Source-The Religion of Peace

INBREEDING

Another appallingly common practice in Muslim communities is inbreeding, whereby first cousins marry each other. A study conducted by the BBC shows that an overwhelming 55% of British Pakistanis are married to first cousins. In Bradford (in West Yorkshire, England), this upsurges to 75%. British geneticist, Professor Steve Jones, has warned against health risks to children whose parents are first cousins are ten times more likely to have recessive genetic disorders, such as mental retardation, significantly diminished IQs, physical defects (deafness, blindness, and infant mortality). Another estimate shows that almost half of all Muslims in the world are inbred. In Pakistan, 70% of all marriages are between first cousins, and 25-30% in Turkey. (Jyllands-Posten, 27/2 2009 More Stillbirths Among Immigrants). Blood related marriages in Arabic countries are startlingly widespread.

Consider the startling statistical research on Arabic countries. Up to 34 percent of all marriages in Algeria are consanguine (blood related), 46 percent in Bahrain, 33 percent in Egypt, 80 percent in Nubia (southern area in Egypt), 60 percent in Iraq, 64 percent in Jordan, 64 percent in Kuwait, 42 percent in Lebanon, 48 percent in Libya, 47 percent in Mauritania, 54 percent in Qatar, 67 percent in Saudi Arabia, 63 percent in Sudan, 40 percent in Syria, 39 percent in Tunisia, 54 percent in the United Arabic Emirates and 45 percent in Yemen (Reproductive Health Journal, 2009 Consanguinity and reproductive health among Arabs.).

Study the lives of practicing Muslim families, and you will discover that the above realities are rampant. Some people defend Muhammad's actions as "cultural norms." Nonetheless, his way of life unacceptable for someone who claimed to be the greatest man to walk the earth. A prophet from God must be an example of love, gentleness, and kindness, and help people come to the knowledge of the truth, and not be the purveyor of torture, violence and death.

Chapter Nine

THE SPREAD OF ISLAM

Within a hundred years of the rise of Muhammad, Islam became overwhelmingly powerful and expanded to Europe, destroying countless civilizations in its path. Upon Muhammad's death, Omar, one of his caliphs (successors), attacked countries like Persia, Egypt, Iraq, Syria, the Byzantine Empire, Israel, Lebanon, killing many Christians and Jews. Muslims even invaded the country of Spain, but El Cid defeated them. The city of Tours in the southern part of France was captured by the Muslims, but were later defeated and pushed out by Charles Martel, known as the "Hammer of the Franks."

Add to the list of conquered nations Turkey, North Africa, Saudi Arabia, Lebanon, Pakistan, Afghanistan, and many others, which became Muslim by force of the sword. If you look at Saudi Arabia's flag, its symbol is a sword with the inscription, "There is no god but Allah," meaning "If you don't recognize Allah as the only god, you will know the sword."

Have you ever wondered why Iraqis, Syrians, Lebanese, Egyptians, Moroccans, Algerians, and other Islamic nations, who are not Arabs, speak Arabic? It's because after Islam invaded these countries, the Arabic language was forced upon them. The Persian language was effectively saved because of a man named Firdausi, who wrote the book *Shahnameh* entirely in Persian over a period of thirty years. Not a single Arabic word was used. It was among the works that remained after Islam destroyed many valuable documents.

Dr. Bill Warner, Director of the Center for Study of Political Islam (www.politicalislam.com) Following is the outline of Islamic attacks and conquests, beginning in the 7th century.

7th Century	• The destruction of Jazima tribe by Khalid. • Khalid at the Battle of Olayis, Iraq • Khalid's rapes • Umar's conquest of Jerusalem made Christians and Jews dhimmis. • These are non-Muslim subjects under an Islamic State.

8th Century – Golden Age	• Attack on Hindustan
	   ◦ 26,000 Hindus
	• Armenians
	   ◦ Nobles Burned
	• Ephesus
	   ◦ 7,000 Greeks enslaved

9th Century – Golden Age	• All new churches destroyed • Amorium – massive enslavement • Egyptian Christians revolt over jizyah
10th Century - Golden Age	• Thessalonica – 22,000 enslaved • Seville – Christians massacred • 30,000 Churches destroyed ◦ Egypt, Syria
11th Century – Golden Age	• 6,000 Jews of Morocco killed • Hundreds of Jews in Cordoba killed • 4,000 Jews of Granada killed • Georgia and Armenia invaded • Hindustan – 15,000 killed, 500,000 enslaved

12th Century – Golden Age	• Yemen – Jews must convert or die • Christians of Granada deported to Morocco • India – many cities destroyed, convert or die ◦ 20,000 enslaved in one town
13th Century – Golden Age	• India – 50,000 Hindu slaves freed by conversion • A 20-year campaign created 400,000 new Muslims out of Hindus • Buddhist monks butchered, nuns raped • Damascus and Safed – Christians mass murdered • Jews of Marrakesh massacred, Tabriz-forced conversions of Jews
14th Century – Golden Age	• Cairo riots, churches burned • Jews of Tabriz forced to convert • Tamerlane in India kills as many as 90,000 in a day • India – 30,000 massacred in cold blood • Tughlaq took 180,000 slaves
15th Century – Golden Age	• Tamerlane in India devastated 700 villages • Tamerlane annihilated Nestorian and Jacobite Christians • After 700 years of attacks, Islam captured and destroyed Constantinople
16th Century – Golden Age	• India – son of Tamerlane destroyed temples, forced conversions • Generals built two towers of human heads after victories • Noble women commit mass suicide to avoid sexual slavery and rape

17th Century	• Jews of Yemen and Persia forced to convert • Forced conversions of Greek Christians to Islam • Persia – Zoroastrian persecution increased • India – 600,000 Hindus killed by Aurangzeb
18th Century	• Zoroastrian persecution intense • Jews of Jedda, Arabia expelled • Jews of Morocco massacred • Hindu persecution continues
19th Century	• Forced conversion of Jews in Iran • Jews of Baghdad massacred • About 250,000 Armenian Christians slaughtered in Turkey • Zoroastrians annihilated in Iran
20th Century	• Over 1,000,000 Turkish Armenians killed in jihad

History books tell us about two Golden Age periods of tolerance and multicultural harmony in Medieval Spain and Baghdad under the "benevolent" Muslim rulers. However, according to Dr. Warner's research, in Spain, which was Muslim by 750 AD, Christians and Jews were "dhimmis" on whom a tax was imposed in exchange for protection. Slavery was rampant and the country was in constant war. In Baghdad, Christians and Jews were also dhimmis, Christian women were sex slaves, Islamic philosophy repudiated the existence of physical laws and cause and effect. Islam destroyed about 90% of all classical books. Christians did the translation work of Greek and Latin works.

There were 548 Islamic attacks in Europe at the Time of the First Crusade in 1100 AD. Dr. Bill Warner of the Center for Study of Political Islam.

Chapter Ten

CHRISTIANITY'S DEFENSE: THE CRUSADES

Contrary to some distorted records of Crusades in the Middle Ages, gratuitous aggression was not the impetus for the Crusades. Instead, they were a distressed attempt to defend against the behemoth enemy, Islam. The Crusades, were the West's response to violent and hostile advances by the Muslim forces. Westerners of all stripes and citizenries were not driven into a dangerous East by the prospect of material gain or glory. Instead, they had to preserve and defend the Western civilisation and culture against intrusion of Islam.

Unfortunately some bitter enemies of Christianity, specially liberal professors and teachers along with some Hollywood filmmakers have tried to depict a false picture of what Christianity is and does. Recently, the impression that most of the youth have about Christianity and Christians is that "they are a bunch of intolerant, rigid religious bigots." But the Christians or the Christianity that I know is that they have made the world a better place.

In the 7th century, when Muhammad was waging war against Mecca, Christianity was the faith of the Roman Empire, spanning the entire Mediterranean, including the Middle East, where it was born. It was the central and supreme religion and its followers were prosperous. For this reason, the earliest Muslim leaders (caliphs) made Christendom their target. Under one caliph Islam destroyed 30,000 churches. This would go on for the next millennia.

Shortly after Muhammad's death, the Islamic warriors were quick to subdue the once largely Christian nations of Palestine, Syria and Egypt. The Muslims had conquered all of Christian North Africa and Spain by the 8th century. Asia Minor (modern Turkey), which had been Christian since St. Paul's time, was conquered by the Seljuk Turks in the 11th century. The Byzantine Empire (the old Roman Empire) was reduced to little more than Greece. In Eastern Europe, Constantinople's emperor urgently sought and pleaded for the Christians in the West to aid them in battle. This was the beginning of the Crusades.

After more than four centuries of Islamic conquests, which had captured two-thirds of the Christian world, Europeans had to prepare to defend themselves, their families, their culture and civilisation or else be taken over by Islamists because they were next to be conquered. The Crusades were the resistance. At the Council of Clermont in 1095, Pope Urban II called upon the crusading knights to fight Islam's invasions and commissioned them with two goals. The first was to rescue thousands of Christians in the East, who were being tortured and enslaved by the Muslims. The primary goal of the Crusades was to defend the West against an enemy that was just not satisfied with the countries and nations that it had conquered and it was heading toward the West. Crusades were not the forced conversion of Muslims. Don't let any "Historian" to tell you otherwise. Christianity is not a kind of faith to be forced upon people. Christ never commissioned His followers to go and force people to convert but to simply preach the Gospel and ben an example in love. But Muhammad commanded his followers to kill anyone who rejects Islam and those Islamists were just doing that. The liberation of the people enslaved by Islamists and lands captured by them was the second goal. Just like recently the Western troops had to liberate Iraq and Syria from ISIS and free the people.

Thousands of European warriors committed to a single cause and trailed deep into enemy ground. Many of them died, either in battle or from illness or starvation. Without a leader, chain of command, supply lines, and thorough strategy, the First Crusade was successful. The Crusades had restored Nicea and Antioch by 1098. Jerusalem was recaptured in July 1099. Shortly thereafter, restoration was underway, beginning with the rebuilding of Jerusalem. It seemed the tide that had catapulted the Muslims to great heights was now turning, so the excitement amongst Europeans was profound.

In the territories won by Crusaders, Muslims were allowed to keep their property, livelihood, and religion. Unlike the Islamists who forced, plundered and killed their subjects.

It's important to note that Islam was dominant in the medieval world. The Crusades were the "counter-culture," an attempt to reverse the trend of Islam. Unfortunately, only the first of many Crusades over five centuries was successful in stifling the military might of Islam.

By the latter part of the 12th century, Crusading had turned into a war initiative. The call to service was issued to everyone including the weak and poor. For the defense of the Christian East, Warriors were asked to sacrifice their wealth and if necessary, lay down their lives. At home, Christians supported the Crusades through prayer, fasting and alms, but the strength of the Muslims advanced. Preaching jihad against the Christians, the great unifier Saladin had solidified the Muslim Near East into one entity. His forces annihilated the joint armies of the Crusaders in Jerusalem at the Battle of Hattin in 1187. Vulnerable Christian cities were forced to abdicate and yield, ending in the surrender of Jerusalem in October 2. Only a few ports held out.

Emperor Frederick I Barbarossa of the German Empire, King Philip II Augustus of France, and King Richard I Lionheart of England led the Third Crusade in response. It was a determined effort but perhaps not quite as resolute as Europeans had expected. While crossing a river on horseback, Frederick drowned. His army returned home. Philip and Richard came by boat, but their disagreements did not help the already problematic situation in Palestine. The king of France returned home after Acre was recaptured, leaving the Crusade in Richard's capable hands. Richard's skill, gifted leadership, and tactical genius led the Christian forces to multiple victories, eventually reconquering the entire coast. After two failed efforts to secure supply lines to the Holy Land, Richard halted his efforts. He reached a truce with Saladin that granted free access to Jerusalem for unarmed travelers and ensured peace in the region.

Although the Crusades of the 13th century were larger, better planned and better financed, they too failed. The fourth Crusade (1201-1204) collapsed under the weight of Byzantine politics. They detoured to Constantinople to get behind an imperial claimant who promised to reward their support by providing support for the Holy Land. But once on the throne of the Caesars, their benefactor couldn't pay what he promised. Betrayed by the Greeks, the Crusaders attacked and captured Constantinople in 1204, the supreme Christian city in the world.

The later 13th century Crusades fared better. The Fifth Crusade, which ran from 1217 to 1221 led to capture of Damietta in Egypt, albeit it was short-lived as the Muslims overpowered the army and took over the city. The first of two Crusades that St. Louis IX of France led, also regained Damietta, but he was no match for the Egyptians and forced to flee the city. Louis was in the Holy Land for a number of years but his most cherished hope to free Jerusalem never happened. Louis had aged in 1270 when he led his second Crusade to Tunis. There he died of a disease that gravely minimized the camp. After his death, the Muslim leaders Baybars and Kalavun carried out a ruthless jihad against the Christians in Jerusalem. The Muslims killed and expelled the last of the Crusaders by 1291, finally obliterating the Crusader kingdom in its entirety.

Muslim power grew in the 14th, 15th and 16th centuries. The Ottoman Turks amalgamated Islam as they conquered fellow Muslims and moved towards the West, eventually seizing Constantinople and advancing in Europe. The Crusades became dire efforts to save what was left of Christendom by the 15th century. It dawned on Europeans that Islam could potentially achieve its goal of subjugating the entire Christian world. In 1480, Sultan Mehmed II conquered Otranto to position his invasion of Italy.

Rome was emptied, but the Sultan and his design perished almost immediately afterwards. It is almost certain that the Turks would have taken Vienna in 1529 with Suleiman the Magnificent at the helm, had rainstorms not delayed his advancement and kept him from taking much of his weaponry. Germany would have been next in line.

Meanwhile, the Renaissance was taking shape in Europe. It was an extraordinary event unlike anything in human history, as Roman values, medieval virtue and a healthy regard for trade and a mindset toward business start-ups combined to bring forth other movements like humanism, the Scientific Revolution and the Age of Exploration. Europe was not only fighting for its life but also gearing up for global expansion.

The Catholics went on to fight, as the Protestant Reformation denounced the papacy and the Crusades. Although such military triumphs were rare, the Ottoman armada was defeated at Lepanto by a Holy League Crusade in 1571. With Europe's wealth and power flourishing, the once great and powerful Turks suddenly seemed regressive and pitiful, resulting in their threat and economy being significantly defused. The Ottoman Empire struggled until its demise in the 20th century and in its wake is the current confusion of the modern Middle East.

Christendom support for the Crusades was far from universal, whereas Medieval Islamic expansion through violent jihad was endorsed by Islamic scholars, as mandated by the Quran. Anyone who has drawn a moral equivalence between the *offensive* Islamic raids and the *defensive* Crusades ought to re-examine the facts and data.

Whether we approve of the Crusades or not, it cannot be denied that the world as we know it today wouldn't exist without the Crusaders' resolute efforts. Thank God that respect for women and aversion to slavery, which were characteristic of the ancient Christian faith, not only endured but thrived.

Chapter Eleven

THE MISSION OF ISLAM

The mission of Islam is to take over the world and implement Sharia law. Majority of Muslims believe their utopia will emerge when the world submits to Allah and obeys Islam. Resist and you might lose your head. One Islamic terrorist group stated, "Inshallah we will soon fly our flag on the top of the White House." This might sound like a joke, but I take it very seriously.

Perhaps by default A similar encounter took place when I recently visited St, Louis. As I left the airport in a cab, the driver quickly launched into a tirade about Americans. He was a Muslim man from Somalia. He was taken aback upon learning I'm a Christian. It's simply foolish to think that assimilation and peace are their ultimate goal because 1,400 years of history indicates otherwise.

I experienced the same thing when I traveled to St.Thomas Island. All of the cab drivers were Palestinian Muslims with long beard who also had Palestinian flag on their cars's window. They were very radical and were playing Quran very loudly in the public close to their cab station.

If the Muslims consider the Quran sacred, and in it they are commanded to slaughter Christians and Jews, is it any wonder that hatred towards both groups and their systematic annihilation are the natural by-product?

Further, note that at least 109 verses in the Quran speak of wars, death and violence against unbelievers, some of which commission Muslims to kill and conquer, which a true Muslim must do.

> **Surah 2:216**
> **"Killing is prescribed upon you while it is hateful to you. But perhaps you hate a thing and it is good for you; and perhaps you love a thing and it is bad for you. And Allah knows, while you know not."**

> **Surah 2:244**
> **"Kill in the cause of Allah and know that Allah is hearing and knowing."**

The above verses suggests killing must be carried out for Allah's sake. One may not like it, but understand that killing is actually a good, righteous thing, perhaps in the same way a physician might prescribe bitter medicine to correct a condition or illness. In the English version, the translators toned it down by translating the word "killing" to "fighting." This has happened frequently in the English translations of the Quran.

A true Muslim must obey the teachings of the founder of Islam. What are the evidence and documents upon which leaders of the free world base their belief believe that Islam is peaceful? Are they going by the behaviors of benign "moderate" Muslims? Would you snack on a handful of M&Ms if you knew that three pieces contained cyanide?

The unrelenting terrorist attacks, jihads, Arab Spring, and revolutions in Islamic countries that the daily news bombards us with are the concerted efforts of serious Muslims to establish an Islamic Caliphate in the world. Under this ruling, everybody will be forced to live according to Islamic Sharia law. This is not the goal of a few self-motivated radical Muslims, but rather the overarching mission of Islam that has been in the works for centuries. Islam has destroyed civilizations and caused the same calamitous conditions everywhere it has gained foothold over the centuries, and it's still covetous for the whole world at any cost.

No example of such hatred is more abhorrent than the Nazi regime's World War II extermination of six million Jews under the auspices of the Muslim Mufti of Jerusalem, Amin al-Husseini, whose assurance to Hitler was: 'We have the same agenda, to eradicate Jews worldwide.' He helped Hitler's cause by recruiting soldiers from Bosnia who joined the dreaded armed wing of the SS. Al-Husseini said, 'Kill the Jews wherever you find them, this will please Allah, history, and religion.' Today, Islam calls the Jews pigs and monkeys, and vows to kill them. This same anti-Semitic rhetoric has cost many lives throughout the ages.

Force and violence are the rudiments of Islamic takeover, but when radical groups realize their survival hinges on cooperating with other nations, certain compromises are made. For example, the revolution in Iran started violently with the leadership trampling upon human rights. At the outset, their words and actions were indifferent to the rest of the world's scrutiny and judgment. However, after many economic and political sanctions were imposed by other countries as a consequence of the Islamic regime's supremacist threats, they started leaning towards moderation. But again, this sort of compromise leaves other Muslims unhappy and at risk of starting another revolution, because they think their government is softening on Islamic values.

Muslims are either slaughtering Christians, Jews and non-Muslim groups in droves around the world, or requiring them to pay a tax to spare their lives. In Islamic countries, non-Muslims have no rights and cannot hold any political office or any other position of influence. In Iran, for example, Christians and Jews have no place in public office. Jewish and Armenian delegates in the Parliament are just for show. They have no real power or influence whatsoever.

Make no mistake - they have been on a mission centuries in the planning and execution. The majority of of Muslims are doing what they believe Allah has mandated. The fact that Westerners and liberals don't believe them or take them seriously is mind-boggling to me. Quite bluntly, as long as Islam exists, there will be terror, fighting, and war.

Chapter Twelve

ISLAM'S PLAN FOR THE WORLD

"We will take over Europe without a bullet. We will take over Europe with mass immigration."
· *Muammar Gaddafi*

In his interrogation, Khalid Sheikh Mohammed, the mastermind of 9/11, was asked about jihad and the plan of Islam. He replied, 'The West's civil liberty, acceptance, openness, and willingness to be responsive and tolerant to other people's culture and belief are actually weaknesses and flaws that Allah has put in American and European cultures, so Muslims can take over.' He said, 'The main strategy to win the long battle is through immigration and outbreeding the non-Muslims.'

Mohammed also said the easiest way to win the battle was for "likeminded jihadi brothers [to] immigrate to the Western democracies and the U.S., and wrap themselves in the Western's civil liberty for protection, and support themselves with their welfare system, while they spread their jihadi message, and then when the time is right they will rise up and attack."

It was a huge mistake by the Obama Administration to withdraw from Iraq. It resulted in mass executions. Obama and liberal European leaders sympathized and wanted to admit hundreds of thousands of Muslim refugees into their countries. I understand we must help refugees, but why haven't these liberal leaders done anything to fight the root of the problem? Why don't Arab countries take refugees with whom they share the same language, culture, values, religion, etc.? Why don't liberal leaders ask Saudi Arabia, Qatar, United Arabic Emirates, Kuwait, Bahrain, Oman, Yemen and other Muslim nations to take some of these refugees? It would be easier, faster, and more fiscally responsible.

Well, because the plan of Islam is to overrun Western civilization just as Gaddafi forewarned, and liberals are paving the way for this to happen.

In the following verse, Mohammed is prescribing the treatment for unbelievers and asking his followers to show no mercy, even to non-practicing Muslims, if they don't pick up arms and emigrate for the cause of Allah.

> **Surah 4:89**
> **"They (Muslim hypocrites) wish you would disbelieve as they disbelieve, so you would be alike. So don't take from among them friends until they emigrate for the cause of Allah. But if they turn away, then seize them and kill them wherever you find them and take not from them any friend."**

> **Quran: 3:151**
> **"Soon shall We cast terror into the hearts of the Unbelievers, for that they joined companions with Allah, for which He had sent no authority".**

In the section on the history of Persia, I described how the great Persian Empire fell into Muslim hands, who destroyed it and left behind a heap of ashes and beheaded bodies. But how did they do so? Small groups of Muslims started attacking Iran from the southwest. The Sassanid king was at war with the Greeks and was distracted from the true threat, and the Muslims took over little by little until it was too late to act. As a consequence, Persia was conquered by Omar ibn e Khataab and many were killed. The same thing happened in Iraq, Egypt, Lebanon, Turkey, and other countries. Islam effectively left the Persian Empire in ruins from which it never recovered. Persian kings had come and gone since the time of King Cyrus until 1979 when Islam took the reins again.

I have personally lived through most events cited in the pages of this book. I'm the voice of millions who are the victims of a duplicitous ideology. Obviously, any of my claims relative to historical or current events can be easily "fact-checked" on the Internet or plugging into social media. There is no way to hide the cruelty that Islam has inflicted upon peoples of many nations. Millions are refugees and forcibly displaced as I write, not because of some "radical Muslims", but because of Islam. Women are subjugated to inhumane treatment and laws because of core Islamic teachings.

In the following verse, Allah asks Muhammad to kill for the cause of Islam and to encourage others to do so also. When Muslims immigrate to the Western countries, as a religious minority, not only are they susceptible to the influence of Muslim clerics, but easily roused to fight for the cause of Islam. Muslims are constantly jihad-conscious, especially where they are a minority because they must put up a fight, "struggle" to adhere to their own faith, and not submit to the kaffir's sway.

> **Surah 4:84**
> **"So kill, [O Muhammad], in the cause of Allah; you are not held responsible except for yourself. And encourage the believers [to join you] that perhaps Allah will restrain the [military] might of those who disbelieve. And Allah is greater in might and stronger in punishment."**

ISIS and other terrorist groups have committed some of the most atrocious acts against humanity. They have burned people alive, drowned them in cages, and killed them in bomb explosions. We have seen videos of beheadings, mass shootings, and their other revolting methods of killing. Images of hundreds of bodies in mass graves are seared in our minds. Their irreverence and complete disregard for human life is unnerving. It seems they enjoy inflicting pain and torturing people. If this isn't evidence of a satanic spirit in and among them, then I don't know what is.

This pandemic is infecting the entire world. I say it with regret that by the time you read this book, many other attacks will have occurred and many lives will have been lost.

MASS MIGRATION

Should we allow the migration of Muslims from war-stricken countries where the lack of sound government and leadership doesn't allow for cooperation with American agencies in enforcing proper vetting protocols?.While Muslim clerics in America and Europe are openly encouraging and promoting jihad, and abusing democratic freedoms to advance their agenda.

A Pew Research Center study asserts that should current demographic trends continue, by 2050, "the number of Muslims will nearly equal the number of Christians around the world." Further, "in Europe, Muslims will make up 10% of the overall population." The study also states that "Muslims will be more numerous in the U.S. than people who identify as Jewish on the basis of religion."

Consider the Muslim refugees. After they come to the Western countries, they enter the welfare system, and become an unnecessary charge to the host nation. It doesn't take long before they start working to establish Sharia law, which caused them to leave the impoverished and violent conditions in their homeland in the first place. Westerners welcome refugees with open arms and give them the same rights as citizens of the host countries. These migrants receive free food, shelter, and medical assistance, yet they later speak against the Westerners as oppressors or worse, kill them as a service to Allah. At this time, there are neighborhoods in London, Paris, and Malmo, to name a few, that are off-limits to non-Muslims (otherwise known as No Go Zones). If you are the only non-Muslim in such territories, expect your car to be broken into, and names and curses painted on your apartment walls. It's akin to being a "Good Samaritan" to a poor, abandoned and weak stranger. You allow him to stay in your home for several days, during which time you feed, clothe and nurse him back to health. But after he has earned your trust, and just before you're ready to see him off, he destroys, ransacks your home, and flees.

The case of one Syrian refugee in Germany who has sixteen children is well-documented. He receives more than €30,000 per month in government assistance. Imagine the economic burden on the taxpayers. Additionally, according to the Gatestone Institute, "although polygamy is illegal in Britain, the state effectively recognizes the practice for Muslim men, who often have up to four wives (and in some instances five or more)." In 2013, the rules changed in favor of polygamous couples in that the additional wives became eligible to claim a full single person's allowance, while the original married couple would still receive the standard married person's allowance. Many Muslim migrants avoid paying government taxes by working "under the table".

This is now happening in the U.S. and Europe as Muslim communities are formed. Eventually they will have military power and voting rights. Soon they will implement their own laws, which are contrary to the Western way of life and human rights. When the West puts its foot down, there will be riots, civil war, bloodshed... Muslims would demand their own land and sovereignty. The West must be vigilant about mass Muslim immigration and monitoring Muslims communities, not because it hates Muslims or discriminates against them, but because it's necessary to protect the laws and liberties of the host countries.

Muslims are indeed welcome in Western countries, but not to bring their own laws, rules, and way of life from which they once fled. The

Boston bombers came to the U.S. as refugees and the government helped them rebuild their lives, but later on, they repaid America by blowing up innocent people. Moreover, in 2016 the Orlando shooter whose family came here as refugees to flee Sharia law not only advocated for it in the U.S., but punished "infidels" by killing forty-nine people and wounding fifty-eight others in a nightclub. In recent years, the FBI cracked down on many Somali refugees and mosque leaders in Minnesota who supported Islamic terrorist groups by providing financial aid or recruiting Somali-Americans for groups like the al-Shabab.

What I describe here is the reality around us and in other nations. Apart from the economic ramifications, the statistics related to violence are alarming. For example, according to the Gatestone Institute, four decades after the Swedish parliament decided to shift from a homogenous Sweden to a diverse and multicultural country (with majority of the migrants flooding in from Islamic countries), violent crime has skyrocketed by 300% and rapes by 1,472%. Sweden, now the "Rape Capital of the West," is number two on the list of rape countries, exceeded only by Lesotho in South Africa. Europeans open their arms and homes to the Muslim refugees and the result of the careless policy and naiveté has been bloodshed.

After the September 2016 jihad bombing in Chelsea, New York, that injured thirty-one people, London's Muslim mayor, Sadiq Khan, said such attacks were "part and parcel" of life in a big city. He added, "It is a reality I'm afraid that London, New York, other major cities around the world have got to be prepared for these sorts of things." This is unconscionable. We cannot accept Islam's agenda as "part and parcel" of our daily lives in the West.

ISLAM'S ALLY: LIBERALISM

In June 2009, former President Obama said, "Islam has contributed to Western civilization." Well, you were just apprised of Islam's "contribution" to Iran - death, destruction, and division. Islam turned the initiator of human rights under Cyrus the Great into the second worst violator of human rights. History is the greatest predictor of what's to come. There is no reforming Islam. It seeks only to continue its ruinous path. I have no idea upon what source President Obama based his above comment.

Many times, various organizations, NGOs, and other groups yield to "political correctness" and effectively compromise in approaching the reality of Islam. Moreover, they don't have enough knowledge about the matter and their understanding about Islam is superficial. Not only that, there are many liberal organisations that actually defend Islam and its inhumane sharia law. In 2017 I testified in Senate Montana against Islamic Sharia law and Organisations like ACLU and some college campuses were defending sharia law! The bill passed both House and Senate Judicial committee and later passed by both House and Senate chambers but was vetoed by liberal Democrat governor of Montana.

Since 9/11, many leaders and politicians have tried to salvage the crashed reputation of Islam by saying it's a "peaceful religion that some radical people have hijacked to fulfill their own personal desires." This statement is wrong and doesn't make any sense. I believe the opposite is true: Islam has hijacked people's hearts and minds to fulfill its desire and advance its agenda.

The Islamists have carried out 32,293 terrorist attacks by 12/29/2017 since 09/11/2001. According to a Jihad record by "The religion of peace" website only in November of 2017 killed 2,013 and 1,123 got injured in 133 attacks, 20 suicide bombing in 20 countries. You can see the details at the end of the book.

Source-The Religion of peace.

The liberal left and media keep drilling the message that Islam is peaceful, which only adds to our problem. Former President Obama once said, "The West is indebted to Islam." He was wrong. According to

Senator Bernie Sanders, another liberal, "The main cause of terrorism is global warming!" Can you wrap your head around this utter nonsense? These are representative of the upper echelon of our society, the elite and educated ones. They conveniently ignore 1,400 years of destruction by Islam and attribute terrorism to global warming!

Other liberals argue that poverty, the lack of education, and unemployment create groups like ISIS and fuel their growth. I beg to differ. The most successful Islamic jihadi plots to date were crafted and carried out by highly educated and wealthy Islamic leaders, of whom Osama Bin Laden is a prime example. According to a World Bank report, "The proportions of [Islamic State] administrators but also of suicide fighters increase with education. Moreover, those offering to become suicide bombers ranked on average in the more educated group." The report further states, "An important finding is that these individuals [from a leaked database of 331 Islamic State recruits] are far from being uneducated or illiterate. Most claim to have attended secondary school and a large fraction have gone on to study at university." Also, most of them were employed before traveling to join the Islamic State. Shocker.

You might have heard the speech of Mr. Khizr Khan (who lost a son in the Iraq war), at the 2016 Democratic National Convention, in which he opposed then presidential candidate Donald Trump for his proposal to ban some Muslim immigration into the U.S. Khan challenged Trump and questioned "whether he has read the U.S. Constitution"! Why is the abundance of evidence not enough to convince people of the perils we face? Why haven't the blinders come off? Who is right here? People are justifiably concerned about their families' security. Soon after Trump became President, he issued an executive order to temporarily suspend immigration from seven Muslim-majority countries, which was repeatedly blocked by liberal judges. Fortunately, months later the Supreme Court lifted the injunctions and green-lit Trump's travel ban.

Islam's love affair with liberals is as strange as it is dangerous to the West. It would seem that Islam and liberalism are a contradiction in terms.

After all, liberals claim to protect equal rights across the board, especially among minorities. Yet somehow they're unfazed by the fact that women are debased in Muslim cultures, or that homosexuals are brutally killed. But perhaps it's not as much as mystery as it seems. Many people in both groups are entrenched in, and operate from, a place of victimhood, of the belief that their misfortunes and inability to get ahead in life are the fault of an oppressive and abusive "other," but never themselves. In this regard, they do see eye-to-eye and speak the same language of misery. To empower each other, they must tear down and destroy others who don't share their values and impede their perceived entitlements.

Do you remember when Palestinian Muslims wanted the Gaza Strip so badly? Under Israel's rule, Gaza had become a paradise, a tourist attraction with schools, hospitals and beautiful beaches where jobs abounded. Muslims demanded the land as the condition for peace, and under the pressure of the international community, Israel gave them the land in 2005. Muslims quickly turned it into a terrorist haven. Rockets are fired regularly at Israel. Infrastructure is destroyed, beaches are dirty and unsafe, tourism is dead, and jobs are gone. Again, Muslims are poor and miserable. They do it to themselves and blame others. True to form, Muslims are always going to assume the victim's role and view Westerners as the reason for their misery, just as Palestinians view Israel as the reason for theirs.

Muslims see Israeli's prosperity in Jerusalem and Tel Aviv, and they want those lands as well. They are convinced that taking those territories would lead to a better life for their people, yet the same scenario will be repeated. The land is merely an excuse. The root is Islam's hate toward the Christians and the Jews, and zero tolerance for unbelievers. In fact, non-Muslims are forbidden from travelling to the city of Mecca in Saudi Arabia. What if Muslims were forbidden from traveling to Denver or Detroit?

The government's primary duty is to ensure the safety of the people and protect them from foreign intruders and enemies. It's not the government's duty to decide on healthcare, education, and business. The Islamic revolution succeeded because Khomeini, along with communist and socialist leaders, demonized the Shah, and convinced a large number of people of entitlements to free education, food, and other unearned benefits, etc. (By the way, after Khomeini assumed power and had no more use for the "leftists" that helped him get there, he brutalized and killed them as well.)

I see a similar situation unfolding in the West now in that political leaders in the U.S. and in Europe feeding on people's dependency and vulnerability by promising to deliver free education and healthcare, welfare and other entitlements, redistribution of wealth (the Robin Hood complex), and justice for all. This happens when governments try to replace God as the people's provider, guide, healer, and the fulfillment of all their needs.

In the West, communist, socialist and liberal groups portray corporations and the rich as opportunistic capitalists that exploit the poor. This is exactly one of the tactics that Muhammad, Khomeini, and other Islamic leaders in the Middle East used to brainwash their people who eagerly bought into the lies and false promises. They sold their values for handouts. They failed to consider their children's future. Instead, it was greed and selfishness for the moment. The prevailing mentality was, "What can I get? I want more. I'm entitled to other people's money."

After the Islamic regime came to power in Iran, they sequestered the people's guns. Sound familiar? Gun control is a prerequisite for dictatorships to thrive, and now leftist groups in America are doing everything in their power to disarm citizens, enforce stricter gun regulations, and ultimately repeal the Second Amendment. We might as well surrender to Islam because I can assure you that the disintegration of the West won't be far behind, if leftists succeed in their agenda.

It's unwise to leave a nation's fate in the hands of power-hungry politicians. When the founders of America established this nation, their goal was to have a very small government. "We the people" are supposed to rule by giving authority to our delegates and holding them accountable. The government's function is to serve the people. However, some government programs in America are akin to modern-day slavery in that they engender dependency on a system that must be kept in power in to sustain the demands of its beneficiaries. They are enabling, not empowering, the masses.

People vote for leaders who promise them things, but these are quick Band-Aid fixes. Excessively taxing the rich only limits their ability to expand businesses and create jobs. It may be stating the obvious, but lack of jobs brings about crime and corruption. Dependency on the government is not sustainable. The system will eventually break down and the government would use force to stay in power. Before you know it, you will be standing in long lines for a loaf of bread and realize that you have created a tyranny!

When communism was popular, millions around the world espoused it, and nations such as the Soviet Union, China, Laos, Vietnam, North Korea, Cambodia, etc., put it to practice. However, the West rejected and declared communism illegal. Why is it that some political leaders defend and justify Islam, a far greater threat than communism?

Some liberal politicians are shameless champions and apologists for Islam. In recent months, we have witnessed, liberal student and militant Antifa groups violently oppose and ban conservative influencers from speaking against the dangers of Islam on college campuses and other venues. Furthermore, there is a huge attack on Judeo-Christian values that teach dependency on God the provider. Christians believe that God is their source, not the government.

I'm amazed that the liberals and "lefties" of the world are perpetually deceived. Muslims have outed their plan and strategy to the mainstream, as instructed and reinforced by their textbooks, yet leftist groups still don't believe them. Innumerable ex-Muslims have risked their lives to come out of the shadows to speak against the oppression they have suffered under Islam and to warn the world about its plan. If we don't wake up from the great deception that Islam is a "peaceable religion", we could lose the battle.

CHRISTIAN PERSECUTION

Sadly, Christians are persecuted for senseless reasons even in Western countries. Nurses getting fired because they prayed for their patients, children being prohibited from taking their Bibles to school, and army personnel being banned from praying or using the name of Jesus, just to cite a few examples. In California, a public school sent a deputy sheriff to a 7-year-old boy's home to enforce the school's order on the child to stop handing out Bible verses during lunch. Why do some of the strongest proponents of tolerance persecute Christians, and yet embrace Islam, which at its heart is intolerant and mandates death for those who disagree or hold a different opinion? Why is there discrimination and patent bigotry against Christians even in the free world?

The assault on Christianity of course boils down to a hatred toward Jesus Himself. Many Muslims and liberals around the world are united by their contempt toward Christians. The truth of Jesus and the Cross is offensive to non-believers, period. They consider Christ followers repugnant because of their "exclusive" and absolutist claim that Jesus is the only way to salvation.

Many Muslims and liberals are strange bedfellows in many ways. Indeed both groups are behind some of our day's most repulsive crimes against humanity. On the part of liberals in the U.S., whose staunch activism led to the Supreme Court's decision to legalize abortion in 1973, their culpability in the 58 million aborted unborn children to date cannot be denied. According to the Guttmacher Institute, in 2008 (the most recent year for which data is available), there were 1.21 million abortions performed in the United States. This amounts to 3,322 abortions per day.

Christian pro-life groups are on the forefront of putting an end to the continuous slaughtering of the most vulnerable and defenseless among us.

Islam, on the other hand, is responsible for destroying civilizations and 270 million deaths over centuries of Islamic jihad and raids. According to data gathered by Political Islam, this death toll breaks down to 120 million Africans, sixty million Christians, eighty million Hindus, ten million Buddhists, and hundreds of thousands of Jews, and…they're still at it! Jihad is ongoing. But who's counting, right? Certainly not the liberals.

It seems that the world, for lack of a better phrase, has a bone to pick with Christ and His Church, even as no other group has done more to solve some of humanity's ills than Christians have. They are the ones who venture into poor countries in Africa, the Middle East and Southeast Asia, and serve communities by digging water wells, building schools, hospitals and orphanages; providing food, shelter, and medical care, etc. In contrast, Muslims in Nigeria kidnap, enslave and rape young girls. In Sudan and in the Middle East, Christians are slaughtered every day. According to the Center for Study of Global Christianity (Gordon-Conwell Theological Seminary), 90,000 Christians were killed in 2016, mostly in Islamic countries. Christians are the most persecuted group in the world.

ISLAMIC TERROR ON CHRISTIANS

This is a list of targeted acts of terrorism on Christian civilians and church workers by religious Muslims only in the year of 2017. At the end of the book you can find more lists of Islamic attacks against Christians since September 11th, 2001. These attacks have nothing to do with war, combat or insurgency. The victims are innocent Christians who were specifically targeted and abused solely on account of their faith by those who claim their own religion as a motive.

This is not a complete account of Islamic terror attacks on Christians since much of the violence goes unreported.

Date	Country	City	Killed	Injured	Description
2017.12.24	Nigeria	Mailafiya	6	3	A shooting attack on a Christian community leaves six dead, including a young child.
2017.12.22	Nigeria	Nindem	4	10	Suspected Fulani open fire on a church group singing Christmas carols, killing four.
2017.12.17	Pakistan	Quetta	11	57	Two women are among eleven massacred by two suicide bombers at a Methodist church during a nativity service.
2017.12.04	Nigeria	Numan	3	0	Muslim terrorists kill a Christian family of three, inlcuding a pregnant woman - who was raped.
2017.12.01	Pakistan	Chaman	1	2	Terrorists kill a child at the gate of a Christian community.
2017.11.17	Kenya	Nairobi	0	3	Three children are injured when Islamists fire into a Christian home.
2017.11.13	Nigeria	Wereng	2	0	Two Christians are murdered and then mutilated with machetes by Fulani militants.

Date	Country	City	Killed	Injured	Description
2017.11.07	Nigeria	Riyom	9	3	Nine Church of Christ members are ambushed and murdered by Muslim terrorists as they are returning from a market.
2017.11.02	Nigeria	Gaambe-tiv	3	5	Muslims target and kill three Christians.
2017.10.21	Syria	Qaryatain	128	0	One-hundred and twenty-eight residents of a Christian town are found stabbed or shot to death by the Islamic State.
2017.10.16	Egypt	al-Arish	7	15	Islamists attack a church and a bank, killing seven.
2017.10.16	Nigeria	Nkiedonwhro	29	3	Mostly women and children are among the twenty-nine Christians massacred by Fulani terrorists while trying to take shelter at a school.
2017.10.15	Syria	Bab Touma	4	5	Sunnis send mortars into a Christian neighborhood, clearing out four residents.
2017.10.14	Nigeria	Taegbe	6	5	A Muslim raid on a Christian village leaves six dead.

Date	Country	City	Killed	Injured	Description
2017.10.13	Nigeria	Hukke	2	0	Two Christians are murdered by Fulanis.
2017.10.12	Egypt	Cairo	1	1	A Coptic priest is hacked to death on the street.
2017.10.11	Nigeria	Aribakwa	4	0	A 2-year-old is among four Christians murdered by Fulani terrorists.
2017.10.09	Pakistan	Jhabran	1	0	A Christian boy is beaten to death after refusing to convert to Islam.
2017.10.08	Nigeria	Nkie Dongwro	1	1	A Christian is killed by Muslim gunmen.
2017.09.12	Germany	Berlin	0	1	Two Muslim refugees beat and stab another for wearing a Christian cross.
2017.09.08	Nigeria	Ancha	19	5	Six women and six children are among nineteen Christian villagers butchered by Fulani terrorists.
2017.09.06	Kenya	Lamu	5	0	Five Christians are targeted and beheaded by al-Shabaab....

Date	Country	City	Killed	Injured	Description
2017.09.03	Kenya	Ukunda	2	2	Suspected al-Shabaab members open fire on a church during service, killing two guards.
2017.08.31	Nigeria	Tudun Wada	2	4	Extremists murder a Christian father and son, then kidnap three women and a baby.
2017.08.27	Pakistan	Vehari	1	0	A Christian boy is beaten to death by a group of Muslims.
2017.08.18	Kenya	Maleli	4	0	Three Christian villagers are beheaded by Islamists after refusing to recite to convert. A mentally challenged man is also murdered.
2017.08.14	Afghanistan	Firuzkoh	3	0	Three Catholic Relief aid workers are brutally gunned down.
2017.08.14	Pakistan	Lahore	1	0	A woman is shot in the head for having married a Christian man.
2017.08.13	Pakistan	Lahore	1	0	A 38-year-old man is tortured to death in prison after refusing to renounce his Christian faith.

Date	Country	City	Killed	Injured	Description
2017.07.28	Germany	Hamburg	1	4	A man on a mission to kill Christians rushes into a supermarket and stabs five people, one of whom dies.
2017.07.21	Syria	Hasaka	1	0	A Christian professor is kidnapped and then shot in the head.
2017.07.19	Egypt	Cairo	1	0	Muslim soldiers beat a peer to death on account of his Coptic faith.
2017.07.19	Pakistan	Faisalabad	1	0	A Christian laborer is beaten to death by an angry Muslim.
2017.07.16	Ethiopia	Hirna	0	1	A young man is attacked by Muslims with machetes for evangelizing on behalf of his church.
2017.07.16	Egypt	Alexandria	0	1	An attempted stabbing spree at a church is thwarted by a guard, who is injured in the process.
2017.07.08	Kenya	Poromoko	13	0	Thirteen Christians are beheaded after being unable to recite Islamic dogma.

Date	Country	City	Killed	Injured	Description
2017.07.02	Egypt	Tala	1	0	Jihadis slit the throat of a Christian doctor at his clinic.
2017.07.02	Egypt	Heliopolis	1	0	A 55-year-old Coptic jeweler is shot to death in his home by religious extremists.
2017.06.24	Egypt	Minya	1	0	A Christian artist is beheaded by Religion of Peace advocates.
2017.06.08	Pakistan	Mastung	2	0	A Chinese man and woman are slaughtered in captivity by the Islamic State for 'preaching Christianity'.
2017.05.31	Kenya	Fafi	1	1	Radicals kidnap two teachers from a school and kill the one who is Christian.
2017.05.31	Kenya	Fafi	1	2	Islamists shoot a Christian teacher to death at a school and abduct two others.
2017.05.26	Egypt	Minya	29	23	Christians on their way to a monastery make easy pickings for Islamic gunmen, who massacre twenty-eight - including ten children.

Date	Country	City	Killed	Injured	Description
2017.05.24	Philippines	Marawi	9	0	Nine Christians are captured by Islamic militants and shot to death.
2017.05.24	Egypt	Cairo	1	0	Jihadis slit the throat of a Coptic construction worker.
2017.05.22	Pakistan	Sargodha	1	0	A father of six is stabbed to death over his preaching of Christianity.
2017.05.15	Mexico	Mexico City	1	0	A priest is stabbed to death during Mass by a Muslim convert with mental issues.
2017.05.12	Kenya	Nyeri	2	0	Two Christian quarry workers are murdered in cold blood by al-Shabaab.
2017.05.06	Egypt	al-Arish	1	0	A Coptic minority is shot to death by radical Muslims at a barber shop.
2017.04.29	Germany	Prien am Chiemsee	1	0	A woman is stabbed to death in front of her two children over her decision to leave Islam for Christianity.

Date	Country	City	Killed	Injured	Description
2017.04.18	Egypt	Sinai	1	4	Radicals fire on a historic Christian monastery, killing a guard.
2017.04.15	Nigeria	Asso	12	5	Fulani gunmen invade a village and mow down a dozen residents in an attack targeting Catholics.
2017.04.13	Egypt	Qai	1	0	Radicalized Muslims slit the throat of a 16-year-old Christian during Holy Week.
2017.04.09	Egypt	Tanta	29	78	A suicide bomber blows up in the middle of a Palm Sunday service, taking out over two dozen Christians.
2017.04.09	Egypt	Alexandria	18	48	A Fedayeen suicide bomber is stopped trying to enter a church. At least seventeen innocents are laid out in the blast.
2017.04.05	Sudan	Omdurman	1	0	A Muslim mob invades a Christian school and stabs an elder to death.
2017.04.04	Pakistan	Lahore	1	0	A Christian man is beaten to death by angry Muslims.

Date	Country	City	Killed	Injured	Description
2017.04.03	Sudan	Omdurman	1	5	Several members of a church are stabbed and beaten by a mob. An elder later dies of injuries.
2017.03.26	Nigeria	Mkomon	1	0	Muslim militants shoot a Christian in the head as he is on a swimming trip.
2017.03.20	Pakistan	Sheikhupura	1	0	A young Christian is shot to death by Muslim extremists after refusing to work on Sunday.
2017.03.19	Nigeria	Oshugu	2	0	Muslims attack a church and kill two worshippers.
2017.03.01	Nigeria	Mbahimin	3	0	Fulani terrorists butcher and pull the eyes out of three Christians.
2017.03.01	Nigeria	Lagos	4	0	Muslim radicals are suspected in the murder of a woman and three children at a church.
2017.02.23	Egypt	al-Arish	1	0	Jihadists murder a Coptic man and set his home on fire.
2017.02.22	Egypt	al-Arish	2	0	A Christian man is shot to death and his son burned alive by Islam proponents.

Date	Country	City	Killed	Injured	Description
2017.02.16	Egypt	al-Arish	1	0	A Coptic teacher is gunned down by Ansar Beit al-Maqdis on his way to school.
2017.02.15	Egypt	Arish	1	0	A man is forced to his knees and shot after refusing to deny his Christian faith.
2017.02.10	Somalia	Afgoi	2	1	Islamists shoot a woman and her 11-year-old son in their home for converting to Christianity.
2017.02.08	CAR	Bangui	3	26	A church burning spree by Muslim militia leaves three dead.
2017.02.07	CAR	Bangui	1	0	A pastor is stabbed to death in his church by Muslim radicals.
2017.01.31	USA	Denver, CO	1	0	A pastor working as a security guard is shot to death at a transit office by a 'radicalized' Muslim.
2017.01.26	Trinidad	Arima	1	1	A Muslim teen is shot dead for having a Christian boyfriend, who is badly injured.

Date	Country	City	Killed	Injured	Description
2017.01.15	Uganda	Katira	0	23	Angered by conversion efforts, a Muslim mob enters a church, beats parishioners and rapes fifteen women.
2017.01.13	Egypt	Asyut	1	0	Radicals slit the throat of a Coptic doctor in his home.
2017.01.07	Nigeria	Kwayine	10	0	Ten people are killed when Fulani militants storm a Christian village.

source-thereligionofpeace.com.

Chapter Thirteen

ISLAMIC SHARIA LAW

Sharia is Islamic Law. It is the religious legal system that governs the political, social and moral duties of faithful Muslims. It is what is meant by «Allah's Law."

Every society has its own laws and rules based upon which they govern themselves. As previously noted, the goal of Islam is world dominion. This necessitates the implementation of Sharia law, which is the Islamic law consisting of mandatory rules and teachings upon which Muslims should live and frame their personal and public lives and behavior. It means "the way" or "the path" that dictates how Muslims must worship Allah and deal with people.

The **Quran** is a collection of words that Muhammad attributed to Allah. The **Hadith** is a collection of narrations of the life and deeds of Muhammad. The **Sira** is his recorded biography. The **Sunnah** is said to be Muhammad's way of life, on which Islamic law (**Sharia**) is based.

The Sharia was derived from the Sunnah - the way of life of Muhammad as recorded in the Hadith (traditions). It pulls various Quran verses and historical narrations into an organized body of rules.

True Muslims believe that true justice will only be realized when Sharia law is implemented on a global scale. Because they view the Westerners who have a relatively better life as oppressors and the ones responsible for their misery, they fight, believing they are doing so for fairness and justice.

According to a poll that was conducted in Egypt a few years ago, eighty-two percent of Muslims believe stoning is the appropriate punishment for adultery, and over eighty percent believe leaving Islam warrants death. Note that these Muslims are not so-called "radical extremists" or guerrilla fighters in the mountains, but instead your everyday grocery-shopping city and suburban dwellers. Even if only five percent of the world's Muslims were devoted to carrying out jihad, that's a staggering seventy-five million people who want to behead infidels, stone adulterers, kill apostates, and implement Sharia law! Despite this, we have not seen any serious action from so-called "moderate Muslims" to condemn or stop the atrocities committed by other Muslims. When was the last time you saw a march on the streets by "moderate Muslims" to condemn such groups as Al-Qaeda, ISIS, Taliban and Boko Haram?

I disagree with people who differentiate between radical Islam and true Islam. As an ex-Muslim, I'm giving you an accurate perspective on Islam and its tenets based on facts. Everything I have said so far is from the Quran and has nothing to do with "Radical Islam." **Islam is inherently evil and dangerously radical, and it will continue to cause problems in the world if not stopped**.

As I said, we are not dealing with individuals or any group or organization per se, but instead an ideology. The idea of Islam is that of misusing people to accomplish its evil purpose. You might say, "Well, not all Muslims are radical," to which I agree. However, if you want to be a true follower of Islam, I promise you will be fighting or killing people, or both (and getting killed in the process). Muslims who are not participating in the eradication of infidels don't know what the Quran says, don't have enough power to act on what the Quran requires of them, or are Muslims in name only. I believe if most Muslims knew the Quran more intimately, they would turn away from it. At least that's what common-sense and a good conscience would dictate they do.

Again, you might say, "Well, I have a Muslim neighbor who is good, harmless, generous, etc." This, however, does not make Islam good, in the same way we don't consider communism good, although we may come across a "decent communist neighbor." Many Muslims have never cracked the Quran open. They are nominal Muslims who form the majority of moderate Muslims. They have no idea what Islam teaches, but they have the potential of becoming radicalized.

In what seems like a benign incident, some angry Muslims complained against a school that served them pork in one of their meals. Well, Jews don't eat pork as well, but you don't see them spewing hate and suing institutions up and down! They simply remove themselves from situations that would violate their dogmas. But the desire of Muslims is for everybody to submit to Islamic laws. If you were invite me to your house, I must abide by your rules. I can't and shouldn't tell you how to run your household. Similarly, if Muslims want to immigrate to Western countries, they must adopt a new way of life and adhere to the laws, culture, and values of the host countries.

There are "moderate Muslims" who have not studied Islam and are therefore unaware of its sinister agenda. They have a superficial and cultural knowledge of Islam. When we see "decent, law-abiding Muslims," we wrongly conclude that Islam is good. On the other hand, there seems to be no end to the chaos that we see we see that's caused by Muslims around the world. Moderate Muslims have unwittingly helped Islam find legitimacy in the world and caused confusion among Westerners. These so-called non-practicing Muslims ought to do a deep dive into Islam and Muhammad's life, and read the Quran in their own languages. I know many Muslims who have done so and left Islam.

I once talked to a Muslim neighbor. Our conversation was respectful, until I raised the subject of terrorism and ISIS, Taliban, Al-Qaida, etc., and he quickly said, "Well, they are not Muslims. You know that, right?"

I asked him, "How do you know?"

"The Quran does not teach what they do," he replied.

I continued, "Have you read Surah 9:29?" He shook his head, so I opened the Quran on my phone, and read the verse aloud.

> **Surah 9:29**
> **"Fight (actual text says kill) those who believe not in Allah nor the Last Day, nor hold that forbidden which hath been forbidden by Allah and His Messenger, nor acknowledge the religion of Truth, even if they are of the People of the Book (Jews and Christians), until they pay the Jizya (punishment by paying or blood money) with willing submission, and feel themselves subdued and humiliated."**

He didn't believe I was reading from the Quran, so he looked it up on his phone. Sure enough, the verse was there. He concluded, "We need to ask an imam to explain this to us." Just moments prior, he said there was no such thing in the Quran, only to concede that an imam would have some explaining to do!

Unfortunately, although we live in a free society, we have adopted a "politically correct" culture, in which we don't tell people when they are wrong for fear of hurting their feelings or offending them. We need to disrupt this PC culture and become bold and effective truth bearers, especially against an ideology that poses an existential threat to our deeply held beliefs and values.

If one is being honest, it is plain to see that Islam is far from a peaceful, just, tolerant, and egalitarian.

SUBJUGATION OF WOMEN

The following sections highlight what Sharia *actually says* about important issues. References are to the classic manual, *Reliance of the Traveller*, considered one of the soundest translations of Islamic law.

m3.4 - 3.7 say that a woman may not "conduct her own marriage", meaning that she is not free to marry by choice. A male guardian is required to validate the marriage agreement.

m3.8 says that a woman is not free to choose her guardian. It is assigned by family relation. Once she is married, she becomes the charge of her husband's guardianship.

A Muslim woman may not marry a non-Muslim man (Quran 2:221). An untranslated portion of the Sharia even forbids an Arab woman from marrying a non-Arab man (source).

(m13.4) - *A woman has no right to custody of her children from a previous marriage when she remarries.*

(m5.1) - *It is obligatory for a woman to let her husband have sex with her immediately when he asks her... and she can physically endure it.*

(m10.11-2) - *It is not lawful for a wife to leave the house except by the permission of her husband.*

(m10.11) - *When a husband notices signs of rebelliousness in his wife, he warns her in words. If she commits rebelliousness, he keeps from sleeping with her without words, and may hit her, but not in a way that injures her, meaning he may not break bones, wound her, or cause blood to flow.*

(o4.9) - *The indemnity for the death or injury of a woman is one-half the indemnity paid for a man.*

(L10.3) - *Divide the universal share so the male receives the portion of two females* (Rule of inheritance based on the Quran 4:11)

(m2.3) - *It is unlawful for women to leave the house with faces unveiled*

In 2017, the United Nations elected Saudi Arabia to the Women's Rights Commission whose primary purpose is to empower women and ensure that their rights are respected and regarded as equal to men's. The irony is that Saudi Arabia is the birthplace of Islam and is one of the worst violators of women's rights. As Sharia law demands in Saudi Arabia, women are not allowed to drive or obtain a driver's license. Moreover, women must get a man's permission to do any of the following: travel, get married, get released from prison, and avail of healthcare. Women can neither file legal claims nor rent an apartment in Saudi Arabia. This is willful blindness by the U.N. toward the inhumane treatment of women. It's like putting a cat in charge of gold fish.

I remember one day I was shopping at a grocery store close to my home, and I met two women with their kids. I overheard their Arabic conversation. As it is my custom to meet people of different nationalities and cultures, I approached and greeted them. I learned that they were from Saudi Arabia. I was surprised because Saudi women usually cover their heads, and these two women did not. After exchanging a few words in Arabic, I asked them if they had ever heard the Gospel of Jesus Christ and they said, "No, we don't believe in any religion or any God." This was even more odd because all Saudis are Muslim, so I asked, "Were you not Muslim?" They said, "Yes, but not anymore."

You can imagine how eager I was to hear their story. They shared that they are sisters who came to the U.S. as students along with their husbands. In an argument, the husbands began to beat them to the point of bleeding. They rushed to a hospital and the doctors asked them, "What has happened to you?" The doctors reported the account of domestic abuse to authorities as described by the women whose husbands were later arrested and eventually deported. Apparently, these men had forgotten that they were not in Saudi Arabia. The two women got divorced in absent and applied for asylum. However, do you know that if this incident had happened in Saudi Arabia, there wouldn't have been any justice for those women and no consequences for their husbands? The two women were so afraid and bitter that I could feel their anger.

I stayed in touch with them and later on shared the Good News of the Gospel of our Lord Jesus Christ. I also told them how much Jesus loves them and clarified the great difference between Islam and Christianity. These two sisters began to open up and ask more questions about the Bible. I would open the Arabic Bible on my phone and we would read different verses that revealed God's character in a way they had never experienced before. I also shared with them my own testimony. Later on, I introduced them to an Arabic speaking church.

Even in the U.S. and Europe, Muslims are committing female genital mutilation, a harsh and inhuman Islamic practice. Some Muslims take their underage daughters or nieces to their Islamic country of origin in order to undergo this procedure. More than half a million girls in the West are in danger of this awful practice. Yet a top editor from The New York Times decided the paper shouldn't use the term "female genital mutilation" because the phrase is too "culturally loaded" and widens the divide between the Western world and "people who follow the rite." Can you see how dangerous political correctness is? The media does not even want to use the term radical Islamic terrorism.

How can liberals claim to be for women's rights ignore the oppression of women and minorities in Muslim countries? According to the constitution of the Islamic Republic of Iran, a woman cannot run for president. The candidate must a Muslim man. Saudi women are denied driving and voting privileges, but nobody represents them in liberal feminist circles. Have you ever heard Hillary Clinton criticize the Saudis for oppressing their women? The answer is no because Arabs and special interest groups support the Clinton Foundation. Now we cannot be carried by political currents and remain silent, because silence is complicity and consent.

Many women in Afghanistan have been executed because they were seen in public with men. Under the Taliban rule, for example, women had to wear the burqa at all times. They couldn't see a male doctor to be treated for illness, or go to school. There is no shortage of online video footages and photos depicting unmistakable misogyny and cruelty toward women as Taliban police beat them with a stick, as if to herd them like cattle. The ongoing rape and sex slavery that women are subjected to by various terrorist groups like ISIS and Boko Haram are evils that we must not only speak against, but also put an end to.

In October 2017, conservative author, blogger, and political commentator Michelle Malkin aired an episode of her show on CRTV, for which I was interviewed about "honor killing". It was humbling to have been in the same episode as other anti-Sharia powerhouses like Nonie Darwish, Brigitte Gabriel and Robert Spencer, who also lent their expertise on the subject based on personal experiences and years of research. I described my upbringing in Iran, and the treatment of my sisters, whose activities, clothing, and marriage choices were controlled by the men in my own family, as prescribed by Islamic teachings. Honor killing is a despicable Islamic practice that allows the killing of children, mostly girls (93%) ages 17-36, who have "shamed the family" by disobeying their parents, using drugs or alcohol, engaging in what might be considered lewd and sexually inappropriate behavior, or refusing to marry someone to whom they were betrothed. In the case of Muslims raised in the U.S., something as benign as "becoming Westernized" in speech, actions and clothing is enough to get young women killed by their own families.

Islam teaches that beating and killing one's own "defiant" daughter, sister, etc., usually by her father (and/or mother who helps cover up the crime), restore honor to the family whose reputation has been soiled by the child's "misdeed". As such, this act is not only acceptable and lauded as heroic by Islamic standards, but actually escapes punishment by Sharia law. The U.N. estimates 5,000 honor killings per year worldwide, ninety-one percent of which committed by Muslims. According to Spencer's JihadWatch.org, there are dozens of honor killings in the U.S. per year, and more go unreported. In his first ninety days in office, President Trump was perfectly justified when he immediately ordered that the data regarding honor killings and other gender-based acts of violence committed against women in our country be tracked and released.

The world's silence over these atrocities, particularly against women, is astonishing. Labeled as "culture differences", the international community has done nothing to condemn and hold responsible the governments that implement Sharia law, chief of which is Saudi Arabia. Although they are supposedly allies of the West, the world has remained silent over the way they treat people, especially women and minorities; perhaps it's because they are the number one oil producer in the world and a major financial backer to United Nations.

Are we to sit back until Sharia-endorsed behavior like polygamy, wife-beating, temporary marriages, female genital mutilation, and honor killings become the norm in Western society too? Perhaps then, the West would wake up. But by then force must be used to defeat uprisings. There would be much bloodshed, terrorist attacks, suicide bombings, hostage crises, and the like. Muslims will always see the West as an obstacle and enemy.

FREEDOM OF CONSCIENCE AND THE FREE EXCHANGE OF IDEAS

(o8.1) - *When a person who has reached puberty and is sane voluntarily apostatizes from Islam, he deserves to be killed.*

(o8.4) - *There is no indemnity for killing an apostate (since it is killing someone who deserves to die).*

Acts that define "leaving Islam" and being subject to execution are listed in o8.7. They include:

-2- to intend to commit unbelief, even if in the future

-3- *to deny the existence of Allah... or any of his attributes*

-6- *to be sarcastic about Allah's name, his command, his interdiction... or his threat*

-7- *to deny any verse of the Quran*

-8- *to mockingly say, "I don't know what faith is"*

-17- *to believe that things in themselves or by their own nature have any causal influence independent of the will of Allah*

NON-MUSLIMS (BIGOTRY TOWARD THOSE OUTSIDE THE ISLAMIC FAITH)

(o4.9) - *The indemnity paid for a Jew or Christian is one-third of the indemnity paid for a Muslim. The indemnity paid of a Zoroastrian is one-fifteenth of that a Muslim.*

(h8.24) - *It is not permissible to give zakat to a non-Muslim.*

(e2.3) - *It is offensive to use the vessels [dishes] of non-Muslims or wear their clothes.*

e8.3 says that a non-Muslim may not touch the Quran.

f21.2 says that non-Muslims are not allowed to 'mix' with Muslims at certain events.

g1.2 says that it is permissible for a Muslim to visit a non-Muslim who is ill, but not recommended. (Same with visiting the grave of a non-Muslim relative - g5.8)

(L5.2) - *a non-Muslim may not inherit from a Muslim.* (or vice versa) o1.2 states that **there is no penalty for a Muslim who kills a non-Muslim**

o11.0-11 says that non-Muslim subjects of an Islamic state may live free from harm if they

- *pay a special 'poll' tax (the jizya)*

- *comply with certain Islamic rules, specifically the penalty for adultery (stoning) and theft (amputation)*

- *distinguish themselves from Muslims by dressing differently*

- *keep to the side of the side of the street when Muslims pass*

- *accept a lesser form of greeting*

- *agree not to build new churches or build houses higher than those of Muslims*

The agreement is broken (meaning that the non-Muslim may be lynched) if he breaks the rules, fails to pay the poll tax, " *leads a Muslim away from Islam"*, *"mentions something impermissible"* about Islam, or has sex with a non-Muslim woman.

(o22.13) - *The judge treats two litigants impartially, seating both in places of equal honor, attending to each, and so forth, unless one is a non-Muslim, in which case he gives the Muslim a better seat*

SLAVERY

A large section of the Sharia is devoted to codifying the practice of slavery (k32.0). The Reliance of the Traveller **omits** these rules from the English language translation, perhaps to obscure the comfortable relationship between Islam and slavery. However, parts from other sections address both the capture of slaves and the sanctioning of forced conversion under obvious duress.

(o9.13) - *When a child or a woman is taken captive, they become slaves by the fact of capture, and the woman's previous marriage is immediately annulled.*

(o9.14) - *When an adult male is taken captive, the caliph considers the interests (O: of Islam and the Muslims) and decides between the prisoner's death, slavery, release without paying anything, or ransoming himself in exchange for money or for a Muslim captive held by the enemy. If the prisoner becomes a Muslim (O: before the caliph chooses) then he may not be killed, and one of the other three alternatives is chosen.*

(o9.12) *Whoever enters Islam before being captured may not be killed or his property confiscated, or his young children taken captive.*

o4.9 is one of several rules that establish slaves as property, to be traded as a form of restitution.

o20.2 makes it clear that a slave freed as a method of expiation must be a "sound Muslim."

THEFT

(o14.1) - *A person's right hand is amputated, whether he is a Muslim, non-Muslim subject of the Islamic state*

ART AND MUSIC

r40.1 says that musical instruments are condemned.

(r40.3) - *One should know that singing or listening to singing is offensive* (with the exception of songs that encourage piety).

(p44.1) - *Every maker of pictures will go to the fire, where a being will be set upon him for each picture he made, to torment him in hell* (w50.2) - Pictures imitate the creative act of Allah (when they are of animate beings).

(o17.9) - *It is unlawful to decorate walls with pictures* (generally interpreted as pictures of animate beings).

Source- Reliance of the Traveler- The Religion of peace.

TAGHIYEH

One of the imperatives of Islam is called "Taghiyeh," by which Muslims are allowed to lie and deceive for the cause of Islam and Allah. In other words, deception is fully justified if it helps the furtherance of Islam.

For example, becoming a citizen of the United States of America requires the swearing of allegiance to this country. A Muslim who takes an oath may say "Taghiyeh" (meaning "I nullify what I just said") immediately thereafter. Imagine a Muslim who is in public office as a judge, mayor, governor, or president, and he or she takes an oath. Do you think this person would honor Islam and its propagation, or the oath he or she has taken? Which of the two would carry more weight? It would depend on whether he or she is a true believer in Islam. How would we know whether the allegiance is to Islam or to the oath? A devout Muslim would identify himself or herself as Muslim first, American second.

ISLAMIC SHARIA LAW - INCOMPATIBLE WITH THE U.S. CONSTITUTION

The Islamic Sharia law contradicts the U.S. Constitution, the Bill of Rights and the Declaration of Independence. It is contrary to Western values. The entire Sharia law is against the Bible.

On the other hand, the U.S. Constitution is compatible with Christian values, for Christians drafted it based on Judeo-Christian principles that serve their purpose of defending the people and ensuring justice and equality for all irrespective of religion, age, ethnicity, etc.

Can you imagine a parliament or congress that's controlled by a group of people who believes that Jews and Christians are infidels? Perhaps a prime minister or president who lives by the Quran and obeys Sharia law, and therefore agrees that infidels must be put to death? Name an Islamic country where there is true freedom, where minorities are treated fairly, and women have equal rights? Sharia law subjugates people to the rule of an ideology. It protects an ideology against people, rather than protects people against oppression. Unfortunately, Islamic standards and practices gaining traction in our schools and neighborhoods will not require much more than our silence, spineless tolerance and passive acceptance.

In 2017, I testified in the Montana senate against the Islamic Sharia law. A truly brave woman by the name of Sandy helped introduce Senate Bill 97 (SB97) to defend women's rights, including those of Muslim women who have suffered under Sharia law. Specifically, the bill would have established the primacy of Montana Law by prohibiting the application of foreign law or doctrines when it violates a fundamental right guaranteed by the Montana or U.S. constitutions. The bill passed the senate and house judiciary committees. However, Montana's governor, Steve Bullock, a democrat, vetoed the bill in the guise of "protecting the religious and cultural diversity". He called the bill a "crackdown on Muslims." When did defending human rights and protecting vulnerable minorities against atrocities become a crackdown on Muslims? Nothing could be further from the truth.

Almost eighty people supported the above bill, and the handful that opposed it was from the American Civil Liberty Union (ACLU) and a university. Isn't ACLU a "defender of civil liberty", and shouldn't they be vehemently opposing Sharia law, which forces women to cover their heads and put homosexuals to death? The U.S. Constitution's first few words are "We the people..." In that senate hearing, an overwhelming majority opposed Sharia law, and should have carried the day, but one liberal governor vetoed it. It was a setback for America, but the fight is not over. The American people are smart and resilient; eventually good will prevail.

women are equal to men, How can someone who espouses Sharia law and harbors a hateful religion and agenda thrive in a society that diametrically opposes his or her beliefs and values? Now how can committed Muslims whose faith teaches them enmity toward people of other faiths or no faith, lead meaningful lives in a Western setting where tolerance is paramount to peaceful coexistence? Islam views anybody who disagrees with Sharia law as Allah's enemy who must be subdued or killed.

Since their laws are supposedly from Allah and his messenger Muhammad, Muslims must decide whether to follow Sharia law or abide by Western values. Those who choose to ignore Sharia Law and live by Western laws and values blend into society as peaceful neighbors. If these people want to live based upon Sharia law, then they must fight their way in a society that practices everything against their beliefs. That's when jihad is considered a fight to establish Islamic rule, under which Sharia law can be implemented.

Just after his capture in December 2003, Saddam Hussein told his CIA interrogator, "You are going to fail. You are going to find that it is not so easy to govern Iraq. You are going to fail in Iraq because you do not know the language, the history, and you do not understand the Arab mind."

When I heard this, I said he hit the nail on the head. Islam has shaped Arabic culture. Muslims want to implement Sharia law. They have been reigning by force and have been ruled by force. Democracy will not last a day in Islamic countries.

Calling to mind another example, during World War I and in the years that followed (1914-1923), the Islamic Ottoman Empire killed 1,500,000

Christian Armenians in Turkey (in a failed attempt to expand and establish the Islamic Caliphate). In 1924, Kemal Ataturk, who had a Western mindset, started to lead his country out of the ashes. Ataturk began to rebuild Turkey by eliminating all the Muslim mullahs who were teaching hatred and jihad. He banned Islam and its teachings (and the hijab) from almost every sector of society, including the schools and the government. Ataturk's hard work and keen understanding led to Turkey's prosperity and modernization that the international community of nations respected and admired. Europeans warned the Turkish leader against changing the constitution, but he called them fascist and anti-Islam.

Fast forward to 2017 when Turks voted to change their constitution, giving unlimited and unchecked power to Erdogan, a passionate and serious Muslim. It is unfortunate to see that Islam is regaining power in Turkey today. Once again, the people misjudged the intent and goal of Islam, which are the farthest thing from establishing "heaven on earth." Soon the misguided citizens may be packing and seeking refuge in another country, as the tide of Islamic laws and oppression begins to rise. If Westerners intervene by trying to thwart an Islamic revolution, Muslims would perceive them as a hindrance to utopia.

This applies to many other countries such as Afghanistan, Iraq, Syria, Lebanon, Somalia, Pakistan, which have become victims of Islam. The fact is that no Islamic country is ready for democracy because what it needs is an "inner revolution," a change of heart among its people. They are so used to force and dictatorship that they cannot tolerate democracy. As soon as a democratic government comes into power, other Islamic groups pull it down and replace it with another Islamic iron fist. Because that leader has to use force to keep his power, he inevitably becomes a dictator.

Christians are being heavily persecuted in predominantly Muslim countries. Church buildings are burned down, Christians get beaten and discriminated against and killed. Recently a Christian man was severely beaten by Pakistani Muslims and his only crime was that he drank water close to a mosque and Muslims believe that since Christians are unclean, he "defiled" that place. The true refugees are Christians who are minority in Islamic countries and are being treated miserably.

Chapter Fourteen

ISLAMIC JIHAD (HOLY WAR)

Islam is not an Abrahamic religion as some have proposed this idea. In fact Islam is designed to oppose and contradict the God of the Bible, the God of Abraham, Isaac and Jacob. God's covenant was only with the Jewish people and their father Abraham. To the Jews God promised the coming of the Savior that He would be a light to gentiles as well as the Jews. All the prophets have been Jewish and they all prophesied about this coming Savior. Muhammad was not Jewish. Islam is exactly the opposite. Its purpose is to takeover the world and destroy any other faith that competes with it. Jihad is its way.

Jihad means "struggle" or "holy war" for the cause of Allah and Islam. It is "to war against non-Muslims in order to establish the religion (Islam)."

There are two types of Jihad. **Lesser jihad takes place when the Muslim fights and kills the unbelievers to establish Islamic supremacy and impose Sharia law over the unbelievers.** The Ayatollah Khomeini called for Islamic revolutions and lesser jihad among Muslims worldwide right after he became Iran's supreme leader in 1979.

Islam teaches that the surest way to enter paradise is to commit jihad. That is, to kill and be killed for the cause of Allah. If a jihadist is killed while fighting, he is promised to enter paradise where seventy-two virgins and rivers of honey and wine await him. Even young boys are promised to jihadists who die for the sake of Islam. This is the carnal paradise that Muhammad promised his followers, a sensual place of gratifying the flesh.

According to Islamic Sharia law, it is the duty of every Muslim and every Muslim head of state (Caliph) to commit jihad. Muslim Caliphs who refuse jihad are in violation of Islamic Sharia and unfit to rule.

Greater jihad refers to a Muslim's inner struggle with his or her faith in Allah and his efforts to overcome any resistance to the Islamic ideology. For example, if one doubts Allah and finds the Quran's teachings and commands of war and killing to be unsettling, then he or she must fight to resolve the uncertainty in his or her conscience.

Muslims are taught the Quran from a young age. They are deceived and brainwashed to do as the Quran commands. No wonder young Palestinians and Pakistanis commit suicide bombing, and churches and synagogues are burned to the ground. Millions of Christians and Jews have been killed because Muhammad cursed them and commanded his followers to murder them. Often we hear from Muslim leaders that they want to eradicate the Jews and destroy Israel. Notice the degree of hatred, to the point that they fly airplanes with hundreds of passengers into our office towers.

There are many volumes and books in which the oral sayings and actions of Muhammad (Hadiths) are recorded. One of those who had collected Hadiths was Muhammad al-Bukhari, whose collections are called Sahih al-Bukhari, one of the six major books of Kutub al-sittah, known as "authentic six" in Islam. Six Sunni Muslim scholars compiled these Hadiths in the 9th century AD. Sunni Muslims consider this collection to be one of the most trusted Hadiths. Interestingly enough, 98% of these hadiths emphasize the **lesser jihad** and less than 2% refer to **greater jihad**, including doing good and honoring one's parents.

As we have learned throughout history, nations engage in wars for the sake of sovereignty, freedom, and what they believe is right for their people, until they win or lose. Once the war is over, it's over. But not so with jihad; the war will not end until Islam prevails. This fight has been going on for centuries.

Based on extensive data gathered and research conducted by Dr. Bill Warner (Center for Study of Political Islam), the 548 battles and 19,000 jihad attacks for which the "Religion of Peace" is responsible, precisely follow the jihadist doctrine. In 1,400 years, only 12 decades are jihad-free.

There were many Christians and Jews when Muhammad started his religion, and by the time he took over the city of Mecca, not one remained. They were killed or they fled. Muhammad said in the Quran:

> **Surah 4:1**
> **So when you meet those who disbelieve, strike [their] necks until, when you have inflicted slaughter upon them, then secure their bonds, and either [confer] favor afterwards or ransom [them]until the war lays down its burdens. That's the command. And if Allah had willed, He could have taken vengeance upon them [Himself], but [He ordered armed struggle] to test some of you by means of others. And those who are killed in the cause of Allah - never will He waste their deeds."**

Muslims must kill unbelievers in order to show their faithfulness and pass Allah's litmus test. While in the throes of jihad, Muslims shout, "Allahu Akbar!" meaning "Allah is greatest!" Islamic supremacists believe that the people of the world are idol worshipers who must either submit to Allah or die. They cannot tolerate women in bikinis at the beach. Seeing Christians going to church and worshiping someone other than Allah is gravely offensive. They won't stand for Westerners having a more comfortable and prosperous life. The Muslim's highest calling is not simply to lay down his life for Allah, but more importantly, to kill the infidels in the process.

Almost every nation that has come under the rule of Islam started with jihad and guerrilla fighting. Propaganda was spread and false promises given. Eventually these nations fell. Poverty, intolerance, injustice, inequality, and oppression are what Islam brings when it gets into power. Just look at the flow of refugees into Western countries; 99% are Muslims. It's because of the very teachings of Islam. What a shame to see the United Nations condemning Israel with resolution after resolution, year after year, because Israel simply defends herself against jihadists. **There is not one Islamic country in the world that does not violate human rights or freedom.**

There is no justice in 100% Islamic Saudi Arabia. What do Afghanistan, Pakistan, Egypt, Syria, Iraq, Kuwait, Qatar, Bahrain, Turkey, Iran, and others all have in common? Are they not Islamic and don't they have sovereignty? Why is there so much injustice and inequality in the Islamic world? **Muslims commit jihad to establish and promote Islam, and once they succeed, they ruin that nation and destroy human rights.**

Furthermore, we have seen the Taliban, Al-Qaida, Al-Shabab, ISIS, Hamas, Hezbollah, Boko Haram, the Muslim Brotherhood, and other terrorist groups, involved in events such as 9/11, the Boston bombing, attacks in Paris, San Bernardino, Malaysia (hotel), Belgium (airport); the Egyptian airplane going to Russia, the Moscow (airport), Israel (stabbing of the Jews by terrorists), and many thousands of similar attacks.

In the course of writing this book, there has not been a month devoid of Islamic terrorism around the world. Just recently, a British-born Islamist, who was radicalized after traveling to Libya, committed suicide bombing at Ariana Grande's concert in Manchester, killing twenty-two young girls and boys and wounding many others. Shortly after, another bomb that detonated in an ice cream shop in Kabul, Afghanistan, killed ninety innocent civilians. Days later, a shooting incident killed thirty-seven people in Manila, Philippines, for which the Islamic state claimed responsibility. According to TROP (TheReligionofPeace.com), there have been 1,808 Islamic attacks in fifty-eight countries, in which 13,160 people were killed and 12,863 injured (year-to-date November 2017).

Chapter Fifteen

MOSAIC LAW VS. ISLAMIC LAW

Some people bring up the arguments that Solomon had many wives and that David was involved in many battles. The difference is that God in Deuteronomy 17:17 explicitly instructs Solomon not to have multiple wives. David fought to defend the weak and the innocent against evil armies who wanted to slaughter them. When David caused the death of an innocent man, God condemned his action and punished him for it. David repented, whereas Muhammad killed many innocent people and married multiple wives and justified it by saying Allah allowed him to do so.

The wars in the Bible were to defend the weak and vulnerable against wicked and barbaric armies. For example, when the Israelites who were slaves in Egypt were delivered and set free by the Lord, they came into wilderness and many nations and armies wanted to destroy them on their path to the promised land. One of these nations were the Amalekites who were sworn enemies of Israel. Remember that Israelites were not warriors when they came out of Egypt. Instead, they were slaves who were not trained to fight. They had only worked with plows and dirt to make bricks, but the Amalekites wanted to destroy almost three million slaves who had been delivered from Egypt. Therefore, the Israelites had to defend themselves, as every free nation would, against hostile enemies and invaders.

God never imposed the tough laws about keeping the Sabbath and other laws on the Israelites. However, they had agreed to abide by those rules. They made a bilateral covenant with God. If someone didn't agree with those laws, he or she could simply leave the nation and would no longer be considered in the covenant. However, if they agreed to the terms of the covenant and violated them, naturally they would receive just punishment. This is no more righteous and acceptable than if you or I were to breach a contract and consequently face some form of penalty.

The Mosaic laws were not meant to be imposed on all of humanity. That's why you don't see the Jews force non-Jewish people to keep the Sabbath or to be circumcised, for example. In contrast, Islamic laws are imposed on non-Muslims. The two sets of laws are not even comparable. Islamic laws are offensive, global and mandatory for all people, while Mosaic laws are defensive, protective and for those who choose to believe and adhere to them. Judeo-Christian values and laws essentially gave birth to Western civilization and established cultures in which we can respect one another despite differing opinions. This is impossible in Islamic societies.

Chapter Sixteen

FALSE PROPHETS

"Beware of false prophets, who come to you in sheep's clothing,
but inwardly they are ravening wolves."
· *Matthew 7:15*

When I converted to Christianity and read the Bible, I was astonished to learn the characteristics that set true prophets apart from false ones. Let's see how Muhammad stacks up against the Biblical standards for being a true prophet of God.

Muhammad claimed to be a prophet of God, and most of the teachings of the Quran contradict the Bible. Yet there is not any prophecy in the Bible concerning the coming of another prophet. The teachings of the Quran contradict the Bible in both the New and Old Testaments. Jesus said He had not come to destroy the Torah and the writings of the prophets, but to fulfill them. Jesus also said:

> Matthew 5:18 *For verily I say unto you, Till heaven and earth pass, one jot or one title shall in no wise pass from the law, till all be fulfilled.*

Now we will examine how to judge a true prophet from a moral and spiritual standpoint. The Bible gives us plain warning that there will be false prophets among us, and that's the spirit of antichrist. The antichrist spirit denies the incarnation, crucifixion, and resurrection of Jesus. It rejects the Bible as being the inspired Word of God. Antichrists reject Jesus as being the only way of salvation. We are going to examine Muhammad's life based on some of the traits of a true prophet to see whether he qualifies as one.

The Bible gives us some criteria through which we can examine whether a prophet is from God or not. These traits are:

There are and there will be antichrists or false prophets:

1 John 2:18 **the Bible predicts the coming of antichrists:** *Little Children, it is the last hour and as you have heard that the Antichrist is coming, even now many antichrists have come, by which we know that it is the last hour.*

1. Antichrists deny the Father and the Son and the Trinity:

In 1 John 2:22-23, **the Bible describes the teaching of the antichrists:** *Who is a liar but he who denies that Jesus is the Christ? He is the antichrist who denies the Father and the Son. He that denies the Son does not have the Father either; he who acknowledges the Son has the Father also.*

Muhammad plainly denied God as Father and Jesus as being the Son of God and said in **Surah 9:30:**

"The Jews call Ezra a son of Allah and the Christians call Christ the son of Allah. That's a saying from their mouth; (in this) they but imitate what the unbelievers of old used to say. Allah's curse be on them: how they are deluded away from the Truth!"

2. The antichrists claim that the Bible is changed and it is not authentic.

Muhammad claimed that the Bible is changed.

Surah 3:78.

"And indeed there is among them a party that alter the scripture with their tongues so you may think it is from the scripture and they say "this is from Allah," but it is not from Allah. And they speak untrue about Allah while they know."

3. Antichrists deny that Jesus was crucified for our sins.

Muhammad plainly denied the crucifixion.

Surah 4:157-158:

"and for their saying "indeed, we have killed the Messiah, Jesus the Son of Mary, the messenger of Allah. And they didn't kill Him, nor did they crucify Him; but another was made to resemble Him to them...

4. False prophets don't have true love in their character.

1 John 4:8 *He who does not have love does not know God for God is love.*

Jesus said in Matthew 7:16-18:

> *You will know them by their fruits. Do men gather grapes from thorn bushes or figs from thistles? Even so every good tree bears good fruit but a bad tree bears bad fruit.*

Chapter Seventeen

THE CHRISTIAN FAITH

Man's heart is "sick" and his problem is more serious than any one of us could truly fathom. Imaginations are constantly devising wicked schemes. Jesus Himself said in Mark 7:20-23: *"What comes out of a man, that defiles a man. For from within, out of the heart of men, proceed evil thoughts, adulteries, fornications, murders, thefts, covetousness, wickedness, deceit, lewdness, an evil eye, blasphemy, pride, foolishness. All these evil things come from within and defile a man."*

Further, the Bible says in Jeremiah 17:9: *The heart is deceitful above all things, and desperately wicked; who can know it?* Suffice it to say, man's problem doesn't lie in the environment, but within him. We inherited the deceitful heart from the first man, Adam, when he sinned in the Garden of Eden. He effectively chose the devil to be his ruler with whom he became united. We are God's creation and He gave us a perfect planet to supply all our needs, but we betrayed and turned against Him. We committed high treason against God, and by joining with His adversary, the devil, we brought a curse and calamity upon ourselves. We elected the wrong leader to rule over us.

Notwithstanding the serpent's temptation and role in the downfall, Adam and his wife Eve knew all too well that they had violated God's command not to eat of the fruit of the Tree of the Knowledge of Good and Evil in the garden.

Genesis 3:7-8

Then the eyes of both of them were opened, and they knew that they were naked; and they sewed fig leaves together and made themselves coverings. And they heard the sound of the LORD *God walking in the garden in the cool of the day, and Adam and his wife hid themselves from the presence of the* LORD *God among the trees of the garden.*

RELIGION

often rules

Oxford defines religion as "a particular system of faith and worship." The reason for the thousands of religions worldwide is that every person knows in his or her own heart that they have come short of the glory of God. Himdependent,

Think of a car that won't start and its owner washes and paints the exterior hoping to fix the problem. Meanwhile, it's the engine that needs repair, not the car's surface. Similarly, the rules and regulations that religion imposes on people may engender outward behavioral changes. However, what we need is a change of heart because it's our "inner man" (spirit) that's corrupt. The problem is not only the act of sin, but also the root that produces sin. Therefore, we need an "inner revolution." Fortunately, knowing the root of the problem is winning half the battle.

When I came to the U.S., I was surprised to learn about the numerous Christian denominations and churches. Gradually, I realized that many so-called Christians were not believers in the true sense of the word, but were "cultural Christians" who have inherited a title from their ancestors. Whenever conversations allow for it, I unhesitatingly ask people how they became Christian. The usual response is, "Well, I was born a Christian (or a Catholic)," or, "I went to a Christian school," or "I go to church every Sunday," or "I was baptized when I was little," etc. There's nothing wrong with having inherited the faith from past generations, or honoring Christian values in our homes, but what is sad and dangerous is that many people think this is all there is to the Christian faith.

If for instance you were to ask me for directions to New York from Oklahoma, I would tell you to go east. Someone else might say, "No! Go west." These are two different "paths," one of which is correct (obviously, go east!). The one who says "go west" learned incorrectly that New York is west from the middle of the U.S.

The followers of every major religion claim theirs is the true way, and yet faiths contradict each other. This shows that not all religions can be true. World religions cannot define love because they don't know what it is. Their followers have never seen it and their actions are no different from those of pagans and atheists.

Although we may sometimes find people who appear to be good, our definition of "good" is relative. For example, if you were to compare yourself with an evil person like Hitler, then you seem to be very good (relatively speaking). However, perhaps next to Mother Teresa, who left everything, went to India, and spent her life feeding the poor, building orphanages, and treating lepers, then your "goodness" pales in comparison.

So how would God go about judging you, Hitler, and Mother Teresa? If God allows you into heaven (although you are "less good" than Mother Teresa), then He must also let Hitler in (because he is just "less good" than you). But the Bible says in Romans 3:23 that *"We all have sinned and fallen short of God's glory"*.

If God let all people into heaven, then it wouldn't be that much different from life on earth now, would it? Because people would still be lying, cheating, gossiping, and doing all kinds of vile and evil things, etc.

Sinful man cannot go to heaven because he or she has a dark spirit. You can never take darkness and merge it with light. The darkness would dissipate because light scatters darkness.

THE OLD COVENANT

Most people wrongly believe that God gave humanity different religions, but it was never God's intent to c Since we were in the bondage of sin, nothing and nobody could help us except God Himself. He selected a man in Mesopotamia by the name of Abram. God promised to give him children and make a great nation from his loins, and to bless the whole world through his Seed (Christ). Abram and his wife couldn't have a child, but God promised to give them a child, as well as land and a nation for his inheritance.

> Genesis 12:1-3, *Now the Lord had said to Abram: "Get out of your country, from your family and from your father's house, to a land that I will show you. I will make you a great nation; I will bless you and make your name great; and you shall be a blessing... and in you shall all the nations of the earth be blessed.*

Abram believed God who counted this to Abram as righteousness. It was by faith, not because of anything that Abram did. Abram cashed in this promise when Jesus completed the Word of redemption by His death, burial and resurrection. God changed his name to Abraham, which means "Father of many nations." God gave Abraham and Sarah a child named Isaac. From Isaac came Jacob, and the Lord visited Jacob and changed his name to Israel. Through Jacob came twelve sons, who were the fathers of the twelve tribes of Israel. One of them was Judah, from which we get the word Jew. The Lord continuously renewed His promises to the Children of Israel. Finally, the Jews went into Egypt. They were there until the Lord led them out of Egypt through Moses. *God gave the law to the Jews through Moses.*

The purpose of the law was to expose sin, not to save them. The law was like a mirror that only showed what was wrong with them, but it couldn't fix them. It's unfortunate that some people try to use the law as a means of salvation. The law was given through Moses not to be a means of justification, but of condemnation. The whole purpose of the law was to show people their guilt, to show humanity their own depravity, and lead the people to God's salvific plan in Christ.

The Lord taught the Jews the destructiveness of sin and its price, and gave them sacrificial laws to familiarize them with the blood, forgiveness, and atonement. This was in preparation for the coming of the real sacrifice, real high priest and mediator.

The prophet Isaiah saw this most amazing moment in the history of mankind, God's plan for salvation, and prophesied:

> Isa. 53:1-12
> *Who has believed our report? And to whom has the arm of the Lord been revealed? For He shall grow up before Him as a tender plant, and as a root out of dry ground. He has no form or comeliness, and when we see Him, there is no beauty that we should desire Him. He is despised and rejected by men, A Man of sorrows and acquainted with grief. And we hid, as it were, our faces from Him; He was despised, and we didn't esteem Him.*
>
> *Surely He has borne our griefs and carried our sorrows; yet we esteemed Him stricken, smitten by God, and afflicted. But He was wounded for our transgressions, He was bruised for our iniquities; the chastisement for our peace was upon Him, and by His stripes we are healed.*
>
> *All we like sheep have gone astray; we have turned, every one, to his own way; and the Lord has laid on Him the iniquity of*

us all. He was oppressed and He was afflicted, Yet He opened not His mouth;

He was led as a lamb to the slaughter, and as a sheep before its shearers is silent, so He opened not His mouth. He was taken from prison and from judgment, and who will declare His generation?

For He was cut off from the land of the living; for the transgressions of My people He was stricken. And they made His grave with the wicked—But with the rich at His death, because He had done no violence, nor was any deceit in His mouth.

Yet it pleased the Lord to bruise Him; He has put Him to grief. When You make His soul an offering for sin, He shall see His seed; He shall prolong His days, and the pleasure of the Lord shall prosper in His hand. He shall see the labor of His soul and be satisfied.

By His knowledge My righteous Servant shall justify many, for He shall bear their iniquities. Therefore I will divide Him a portion with the great, and He shall divide the spoil with the strong, because He poured out His soul unto death, and He was numbered with the transgressors, and He bore the sin of many, and made intercession for the transgressors.

THE NEW COVENANT

For the law was given through Moses, but grace and truth came through Jesus Christ.
- John 1:17

There are sixty-six books in the Bible, written by forty different men, and none of them contradicts another, as though one author had inspired them. These men lived in various times of history, and none of them knew their writings were going to be part of the Bible. The different books are like pieces of a puzzle that one puts together, and when finished, depict a whole picture, which is Jesus.

> John 1:14
> *And the Word became flesh and dwelt among us, and we beheld His glory, the glory as of the only begotten of the Father, full of grace and truth.*

Finally, as foretold by Isaiah, the real Savior came. He was born as a baby to a peasant woman in a stable in Bethlehem of Judea. He became a grown man, passed the tests of life, lived a perfect life, and never sinned. Jesus personified God's love, compassion, forgiveness, grace and mercy. He was and is God's love and character in the flesh.

God nullified the first covenant of law to establish the covenant of grace, which is secured by the blood of Jesus.

> Hebrews 10:9-10
> *He said, Behold, I have come to do Your will, O God. He takes away the first that He may establish the second. By that will we have been sanctified through the offering of the body of Jesus Christ once for all.*

The supreme court of heaven had a complaint against us. We couldn't pay our sin debt, but God who was rich in mercy loved us, came, and paid the price.

Romans 6:23 says, "For the wages of sin is death, but the gift of God is eternal life in Christ Jesus our Lord." Jesus knew the kind of suffering, the hell and eternal damnation that awaited us as sinners. Jesus came to save us. He knew we couldn't make it on our own.

Unlike earthly kings who jeopardized their own people in order to secure their reign, the Lord Jesus left heavenly splendor and at the appointed, He was led as a lamb to slaughter, a sacrifice for sin. He came and took God's wrath upon Himself. The creatures beat the Creator. They spat on Him, insulted and assaulted Him, they put a crown of thorns on His head, they mocked and humiliated Him, but He willingly died for us in a manner so gruesome and unfit for the King of kings.

Jesus is the true Passover Lamb and His blood, the atonement for our sins. On the cross, justice was at once served and God's unconditional love and grace were manifested.

Even Jesus' dying words were of unflinching love, strange to the ears of ruthless and selfish humanity.

> Luke 23:34
> *"Father, forgive them for they don't know what they do."*

You might ask, "Why did Jesus have to die? Couldn't God just forgive us and call it a day?' Imagine for a moment a good man who committed murder, for which he was arrested and taken to a court. What if the judge said, "I know this man. He is a good neighbor. He has built schools, orphanages, and hospitals, and he regularly gives to charities. He has made one mistake. I will let him go!" Could he do this? Would he be a just judge? No! Regardless of person's good conduct up until he committed the crime and his relationship with the judge, he must be tried and judged based upon the law of the land.

In the old covenant God gave us some laws to keep but in the new covenant God give us a life that keeps us. The law of sin and death is replaced with law of life in Christ. We obey God from the heart and our good works are the result of our genuine faith not a way to God.

Likewise, God cannot just forgive us without paying the price. If He did, He would be unjust to ignore His own law. The law says that *the penalty of sin is death* (Romans 6:23). *We all have sinned* (Romans 3:23). We must die the eternal death, meaning eternal separation from God. But because

God loved us, He sent His Son Jesus who became a man and bailed us out. He became a substitute for us.

Just as Adam sinned and we became sinners, Jesus died on our behalf so we who believe and commit to Jesus and His sacrifice and resurrection could be justified through His blood.

> Romans 5:19
> *For as by one man's disobedience (Adam's) many were made sinners, so also by one Man's obedience (Jesus') many will be made righteous.*

BORN AGAIN

"Most assuredly, I say to you, unless one is born again, he cannot see the kingdom of God."
- Jesus, John 3:3

As Jesus definitively said, the solution to man's problem is to be born again, from above. He needs new a nature, a new heart and only the true and living God can change hearts. The cure, therefore, for what ails humanity is heart transformation, not merely behavior modification that most religions and modern psychology prescribe. Simply relying on our willingness to do the "right thing" apart from the Spirit of God is no match for our inherent sin nature and effortless inclination toward evil. Our spirit is dark and sinful, and needs to be changed to be able to join the most Holy God. We must become light to join light.

So what did Jesus mean by being "born again"? Nicodemus, a religious leader and teacher among the Pharisees who came to Jesus at night, asked if it was possible for an old man to re-enter his mother's womb to be reborn, to which Jesus responded in John 3:5, "Most assuredly, I say to you, unless one is born of water and the Spirit, he cannot enter the kingdom of God. That which is born of the flesh is flesh, and that which is born of the Spirit is spirit. Do not marvel that I said to you, 'You must be born again.'"

Righteousness (right standing with God) cannot be bought or inherited. Every person must commit to Jesus on a personal level and understand what He has done for us. The Bible says in Romans 10:4, "For Christ *is* the end of the law for righteousness to everyone who believes."

When we become aware of our sinfulness and come to terms with our need for a Savior, and begin to ask questions such as, "*Where did I come from? What is the purpose of this life? What are sin and morality? Where am I going to go after I die?*"

As He says so in His Word, God will reveal Himself to you when you genuinely ask Him to show you the truth:

> Jeremiah 29:12-14
> *Then you will call on me and come and pray to me, and I will listen to you. You will seek me and find me when you seek me with all your heart. I will be found by you says the Lord and will bring you back from your captivity.*

God knows and sees your heart when you seek Him. He then reveals His Son to you and the Son reveals the Father through the Holy Spirit, as the Bible says:

> Romans 10:8-13
> *But what does it say? The word is near you, in your mouth and in your heart (that is, the word of faith which we preach): that if you confess with your mouth the Lord Jesus and believe in your heart that God has raised Him from the dead, you will be saved. For with the heart one believes unto righteousness (becoming right with God), and with the mouth confession is made unto salvation. Whoever believes on Him will not be put to shame. For there is no distinction*

*between Jew and Greek, for the same Lord over all is rich to
all who call upon Him. For whoever calls on the name of the
Lord shall be saved.*

When I became a believer in Jesus, I walked into Christianity by faith, as I knew close to nothing about it up until the moment that I asked Jesus to reside in my heart. The little that I did know prior to that time were lies fed to me by Islam. I didn't learn Christianity in a seminary and inherit it by tradition. I didn't go to a Catholic school and I wasn't brought up in a Christian home.

However, my relationship with Jesus was intimate from the start. I would talk to Him and He would respond. I have since tasted and seen that the Lord is good. I have experienced His unconditional love. I had a personal encounter with Jesus when I first called out to Him. The Holy Spirit has since comforted, taught, guided, and led me in ways everlasting. I never had that kind of experience as a Muslim.

Further, Jesus said:

John 10:27
*My sheep hear My voice, and I know them, and they
follow Me.*

Sinless Jesus became sin and a substitute for us. Jesus came to seek and save that which was lost. He came to bless us. When we hear about the Gospel of our Lord and Savior Jesus Christ and that He left His glory and majesty in heaven, and made Himself of no reputation and was obedient to the point of death, even death on the cross, then we have a choice to either to believe and accept, or reject the free gift of salvation.

In Ezekiel 36:26-27, God said:

*I will give you a new heart and put a new spirit within you;
I will take the heart of stone out of your flesh and give you
a heart of flesh. I will put My Spirit within you and cause*

> *you to walk in My statutes, and you will keep My judgments*
> *and do them.*

My friends, regardless of your race, gender, color, religion, and nationality, God loves you. He is speaking to you through this book. He wants to save you. All He requires today is not a bunch of laws and rituals, but faith alone, a genuine faith that results in a tremendous transformation. The Bible says:

> Romans: 10:8-13
> *But what does it say? The word is near you, in your mouth*
> *and in your heart (that is, the word of faith which we*
> *preach): that if you confess with your mouth the Lord Jesus*
> *and believe in your heart that God has raised Him from the*
> *dead, you will be saved. For with the heart one believes unto*
> *righteousness, and with the mouth confession is made unto*
> *salvation. For the Scripture says, whoever believes on Him*
> *will not be put to shame. For there is no distinction between*
> *Jew and Greek (non-Jews), for the same Lord over all is rich*
> *to all who call upon Him. For whoever calls on the name of*
> *the Lord shall be saved.*

The only thing you need to do is to allow Him to be your Savior and your Lord. If you open your heart, He will come in, forgive all your sins, and you will be saved. When you receive Jesus, you will be born again in your spirit.

If you want to give your heart to Jesus Christ, pray this prayer from the bottom of your heart. Do it genuinely and sincerely. If you do so, all your sins will be forgiven, and you will be born again. You will become a child of God, your heart will change, and you will enter an eternal covenant with God through Jesus Christ.

Pray:
"Almighty God, You who created me, I come to You
today. I confess that I'm a sinner, but I come to You

through the Blood of Jesus. I repent of my sins. I believe that Jesus Christ is Your beloved Son, who has been with You from the beginning, who came into the flesh to die for me on the cross to take away my sins, whom You raised from the dead by the Holy Spirit after three days. Jesus, I accept You as my Lord and Savior. I ask You to come into my heart, be my Lord and Savior, and give me a new life. Fill me with the Holy Spirit, use me for Your glory, and lead me into the truth. In Jesus' Name, Amen."

If you prayed this prayer, God forgave all your sins. You are a brand new person in the spirit. Whether you feel it or not, you have become a new person. You are in relationship with God and you have become His child. Now get a Bible, read it daily to change your mind, put away your old mindset, and walk in love. Find a Spirit-filled, Bible-believing church, which is your new family, and attend it faithfully. Pray every day. Just talk to God like a friend. Tell Him how much you love Him and thank Him for saving you. Tell Him your needs and follow Him. Love Him and worship Him. He is the Good Shepherd. He will heal you, protect you, and bless you abundantly. The Bible says *He casts out our sins into the depth of the sea.* Micah 7:19.

Isaiah 1:18 says:

> *Come now and let us reason together, says the Lord, though your sins are like scarlet, they shall be as white as snow; though they are red like crimson they shall be as wool.*

A true believer knows exactly when he gave his heart to Jesus. A marriage is the closest thing to which I can compare our relationship with God. Just as a man would ask a woman that he has fallen in love with to marry him and enter into a covenant relationship with her, so do we enter a binding covenant and friendship with the Lord when we accept the supreme sacrifice of His son Jesus.

BAPTISM

The marriage ceremony is what water baptism is to salvation. It's not the baptism in water that saves you, but faith in Jesus and what He has done on the cross and His resurrection from the dead. Baptism tells the spiritual realm and witnesses that your old nature, your old person, has died with Jesus Christ and rose again. Just like a natural birthday, we have a spiritual birthday, the day we entered that Holy Covenant with the Lord.

In the old covenant, any male child had to be circumcised to be a part of God's people. It was symbolic of the new birth. In the new covenant, God circumcises our hearts. He takes away the sin-producing machine in us and replaces it with His own love and law. Therefore, when someone genuinely becomes a believer in Christ, he or she will change drastically. We need to renew our mind daily to our new identity in Christ. The Lord prophesied this through Jeremiah and Ezekiel hundreds of years before Jesus Christ our Lord came to the world.

> Jeremiah 31:31-34
> *Behold, the days are coming, says the Lord, when I will make a new covenant with the house of Israel and with the house of Judah— not according to the covenant that I made with their fathers in the day that I took them by the hand to lead them out of the land of Egypt, My covenant which they broke, though I was a husband to them, [a] says the Lord. But this is the covenant that I will make with the house of Israel after those days, says the Lord: I will put My law in their minds, and write it on their hearts; and I will be their God, and they shall be My people. No more shall every man teach his neighbor, and every man his brother, saying, 'Know the Lord,' for they all shall know Me, from the least of them to the greatest of them, says the Lord. For I will forgive their iniquity, and their sin I will remember no more.*

When someone accepts Jesus as his Lord and Savior, he becomes a new creation in his spirit. God takes away the sinful nature from his heart.

> 2 Corinthians 5:17
> *Therefore, if anyone is in Christ, he is a new creation; old things have passed away; behold, all things have become new.*

Inasmuch as the crucifixion and death of our Lord Jesus is the substance of the Christian faith, it was His resurrection from the dead on the third day that brought forth a hope for humanity, and has assured and sealed the promise of eternal life with Him.

Chapter Eighteen

THE EFFECT OF CHRISTIANITY
ON THE WORLD

"Either make the tree good and its fruit
good, or else make the tree bad and its fruit
bad; for a tree is known by its fruit."
· Jesus, Matthew 12:33

The true Christian faith always changes people's hearts. Indeed, the Judeo-Christian faith essentially built the Western Civilization. The list of Christian contributions worldwide is extensive. What I provide below are just a few notable examples of how the Christian faith has richly informed and blessed humanity by helping nations flourish in their ethics and economies over the centuries.

Right after Martin Luther's protest, **Johannes Gutenberg** (c. 1400-1468), himself a Christian, introduced printing to Europe and in 1439 used the first printing press. The Gutenberg Bible was the first major book printed using the new mechanical movable type printing technology. Gutenberg's invention started the Printing Revolution, which was integral to the development of the Renaissance, the Reformation, the Age of Enlightenment and the scientific revolution, and laid the groundwork for the modern knowledge-based economy and the spread of learning to the masses. When the public gained access to the Bible in various languages, and were born again, the Protestant Reformation took place in 1517.

When former atheist and slave trader **John Newton** (1725-1807) heard the Gospel and accepted Jesus Christ as his Lord and Savior, his life changed remarkably. In his famous poem published in 1779, he wrote:

> "Amazing grace! how sweet the sound
> That saved a wretch like me!
> I once was lost, but now am found,
> Was blind, but now I see.
>
> 'It was grace that taught my heart to fear,
> And grace my fears relieved;
> How precious did that grace appear
> The hour I first believed!
>
> Thro' many dangers, toils, and snares,
> I have already come;
> 'Tis grace hath brought me safe thus far,
> And grace will lead me home.
>
> The Lord has promised good to me,
> His word my hope secures;
> He will my shield and portion be
> As long as life endures.
>
> Yes, when this flesh and heart shall fail,
> And mortal life shall cease;
> I shall possess, within the veil,
> A life of joy and peace.
>
> The earth shall soon dissolve like snow,
> The sun forbear to shine;
> But God, who called me here below,
> Will be forever mine.

Notice what God did to transform a slave trader. Unlike religion that only changes behavior, the power of the Gospel of Jesus Christ changes people's hearts. True Christianity is not a religion but a true relationship with the living God.

Englishman William Wilberforce (1759-1833) was a native of Kingston upon Hull, Yorkshire. He became an Evangelical Christian, which resulted in major changes to his lifestyle and a lifelong concern for reform. He was a leader of the movement to eradicate the slave trade in Great Britain. (In contrast, Muslims sold the slaves they captured in Africa.)

It's unfortunate that some people view Christians as responsible for slavery, although they were in fact the ones who actively opposed it. Muslims who sold slaves to the Westerners are now telling African Americans that Christianity is the white man's religion, the religion of slave owners, which is false. Actually, the opposite had happened. Some claim that Hitler was a Christian, also false. In fact, Hitler hated the Christians and imprisoned and killed many of them for hiding the Jews in their houses. Remember that Satan is a liar.

Corrie ten Boom (1892-1983), a Dutch watchmaker and devout Christian who, along with her father and other family members, helped many Jews escape the Nazi Holocaust during World War II. She was imprisoned for her actions. Her most famous book, *The Hiding Place*, describes the ordeal. Martin Niemöller (1892-1984), a German anti-Nazi theologian and a pastor, was among the many religious that Hitler and the Nazis either imprisoned or killed.

Another extraordinary Christian, 16th U.S. President Abraham Lincoln (1809-1865), was responsible for the Emancipation Proclamation that abolished slavery, and paid for it with his own blood.

In recent history, we see Martin Luther King Jr. (1929-1968), an American pastor who was a leader in the African-American Civil Rights Movement. He is beloved for his role in the advancement of civil rights using nonviolent civil disobedience to oppose segregation. He also paid for it with his own blood. Some of his famous quotes include:

"By opening our lives to God in Christ, we become new creatures. This experience, which Jesus spoke of as the new birth, is essential if we are to be transformed nonconformists. Only through an inner spiritual transformation do we gain the strength to fight vigorously the evils of the world in a humble and loving spirit."

"Darkness cannot drive out darkness; only light can do that. Hate cannot drive out hate; only love can do that."

"The ultimate measure of a man is not where he stands in moments of comfort and convenience, but where he stands in times of challenge and controversy."

"Faith is taking the first step even when you don't see the whole staircase."

There are many other history-makers whose Christian conviction was the basis for our just and moral society. On the other hand, African-American and Islam-convert, Malcolm X (1925-1965), also opposed segregation but believed in a violent racial war against white America. He was killed by the NOI (Nation of Islam), an African American political and religious organization. Notice the effect that Christianity had on Martin Luther King Jr., and that of Islam on Malcolm X.

As far as inventions go, it's hard to top what the Wright brothers accomplished. With the encouragement of their father who was a Christian pastor, Orville (1871-1948) and Wilbur (1867-1912), invented, built, and flew the first successful airplane in 1903. It's amazing how their invention revolutionized our world. And there are so many other Christians who, by the help of God Almighty, and the Lord Jesus Christ, contributed to industry.

In the field of education, Christians founded some of the finest universities that have produced world-changers. The University of Oxford in London has been educating people since 1096 AD. Among its notable alumni are twenty-eight Nobel laureates, twenty-seven UK Prime Ministers, and many foreign heads of state. *Dominus Iluminatio Mea* is the motto Oxford, which is based upon Psalm 27:1 and means "the Lord is my light."

The motto of Harvard University (Cambridge, MA) was *Christo et Ecclesiae*, meaning "Christ and the Church," and in the middle of the logo was Veritas, meaning "Truth." Unfortunately, as modern academia rushed toward secularism, they changed the motto to *Veritas* (although on diplomas the complete logo still appears).

In addition, the motto of the University of Berkeley is *"Let There be Light,"* based upon the Bible verse Genesis 1:3. *"Humanitatem per Crucem Alere,"* which means, "To nourish humanity through the Cross" is the motto of Anderson University in South Carolina.

Closer to home, my Christian friend Todd who is a pastor and a teacher, went to earthquake-struck Haiti with his sons during his week-long vacation, to help the poor people rebuild their homes. They did construction work in the heat in the hardest hit areas. Yet at home in the U.S. and abroad as well, they have faced persecution.

Nations such as South Korea, South Africa, Singapore, Europe, Australia, New Zealand, and others in North America have changed for the better as the result of accepting the Gospel of Jesus Christ. I wrote this chapter while on a mission trip to San Juan in Christian-majority Puerto Rico, a U.S. territory. I also spend time in St. Thomas, Antigua, Anguilla, etc., and witnessed firsthand the Christian faith's positive impact on their people.

We as Christians must be steadfast in our faith. We are swimming upstream. We are the salt and light to this dark world. Only by being grounded spiritually can we be strong witnesses of the Lord Jesus Christ.

We must also maintain a holy and a pure life, so people can see our good works and glorify our heavenly Father and the Lord Jesus Christ our Savior. We must walk in love. Jesus said in John 13:35 "By this all will know that you are My disciples, if you have love for one another."

Our highest calling as Christians is to love God and others. We must be Spirit-filled believers, spending time in the Word, praying constantly in the Spirit, fellowshipping with likeminded believers, and growing to be effective messengers in our world. Time is short. Let's carry this message. Let's fulfill our ministries. Let's run the race with endurance.

Chapter Nineteen

HOW TO SHARE THE GOSPEL WITH MUSLIMS

*"But sanctify the Lord God in your hearts, and always be
ready to give a defense to everyone who asks you a reason
for the hope that is in you, with meekness and fear;"*
- 1 Peter 3:15

I was born and raised in a society ruled by Sharia law, under which women are oppressed, human life is devalued, and minorities are treated harshly. Growing up, I saw how Islam destroyed people's lives. Islam s the culture of shame and pride.

Every time I speak with Sunni Muslims and share with them my story, they say, "Oh you were Shi'ite Muslim; Shi'ite's are not real Muslims." But Shi'ites say the same thing about Sunnis. Both groups have the same Quran. As an ex-Muslim, I was zealous for Islam (and I know many Muslims who are), but my zeal was not according to true knowledge. I believe everybody should be open to anyone who challenges his or her belief.

There is a religious event for Shi'ite Muslims called "Ashura." During this event, people mourn for Hussein, Muhammad's grandson who was killed in battle at Karbala in the year 680. They beat their chests and shoulders with chains, and wound their heads with daggers. People also put mud on their heads and walk barefoot on hot pavement.

Most people do these things because they know in their hearts that they are sinners and don't know how to get right with God. I used to perform the same rituals to please God and earn points to go to heaven. I didn't know Jesus back then. I thought He was only a prophet. Now I know that I'm saved by just believing in Jesus Christ and surrendering my life to Him.

> Romans 10:2-4
> *For I bear them witness that they have a zeal for God, but not according to knowledge. For they being ignorant of God's righteousness, and seeking to establish their own righteousness, have not submitted to the righteousness of God, for Christ is the end of the law for righteousness to everyone who believes.*

God only requires faith, not rituals or religious activities. Salvation is made possible only by what Jesus did on the cross. He paid for my sins with His own blood. Oh, how awesome is the grace of God! Salvation is a gift. It is free. I pray all Muslims would hear this good news and come to Christ for salvation and justification by faith.

After WWII, the world-renowned evangelist, Rev. Billy Graham traveled to Europe. He met with the post-WWII German Chancellor, Mr. Konrad Adenauer (1876–1967).

He asked Rev. Billy Graham, "Do you really believe that Jesus rose from the dead?"

Rev. Graham paused for a moment and said, "Sir, if Jesus didn't rise from the dead, I wouldn't have a Gospel to preach. The good news of the Gospel is that Jesus rose from the dead."

Mr. Adenauer walked to his office window and looked outside for a few moments, and then replied, "Mr. Billy Graham, if Jesus didn't rise from the dead, I see no other hope for humanity."

Later on, Mr. Winston Churchill said the same thing, that there is no other hope for humanity.

Christians have been entrusted with a glorious Gospel. We have the living water for a desperate and lost world. We have the solution to the world's chaos. His name is Jesus. He asked us to go into all the world and share this good news with everyone.

> Romans 10:14-15
> *How then shall they call on Him in whom they have not believed? And how shall they believe in Him of whom they have not heard? And how shall they hear without a preacher? And how shall they preach unless they are sent? As it is written: "How beautiful are the feet of those who preach the gospel of peace, who bring glad tidings of good things!"*

Further, lest we forget Jesus' words in John 14:6: *"I am the way, the truth, and the life, no one comes to the Father except through Me."*

Never deny the people the right to hear the Gospel. The Gospel is the power of God to save people from hell.

> Romans 1:16-17
> *For I am not ashamed of the gospel of Christ for it is the power of God to salvation for everyone who believes, for the Jew first and also for the Greek (non-Jew). For in it the righteousness of God is revealed from faith to faith; as it is written, The just shall live by faith.*

Many people in the world are searching for truth. They are lost and hopeless. The Bible says in Isaiah 53:6, *All we like sheep have gone astray; We have turned every one to his own way...*

We are all lost until we find and accept Christ, including Muslims of whom many are sincere, but they are sincerely wrong. There are 1.6 billion Muslims in the world, and not one of them is sure he will go to heaven when he dies. According to Islam, the only sure way for them to get into heaven is to commit jihad, which is dying for the sake of Allah, while fighting the unbelievers. We need to share the Gospel of Jesus Christ with them boldly and unashamedly.

All Christianity is based on the death, burial and resurrection of Jesus Christ, and all Christians agree on these truths. When the Quran declares that Jesus wasn't crucified, they come against Christians because they say that the Bible has been changed. Yet they don't have any documents to prove that claim. During the first century, everybody was convinced that Jesus was crucified. Even the historians confirm that, and there are more than 5,000 manuscripts of the Bible. So if someone wants to change it, he must find all these 5,000 manuscripts and change them at the same time, which is impossible. There are also the Dead Sea scrolls found by a young Muslim shepherd who was looking for his lost sheep. The Bible has more evidence proving its accuracy than any other historical book.

I sincerely want to help Muslims come out of deception, lies and bondage, just like any of us would help a cancer-stricken friend or family member fight off a deadly disease. The truth is often painful, but a patient with a serious illness must be told of his condition in order to receive proper treatment and be healed. Islam is a cancer to the world. This truth is not pleasant to Muslims, but if we really love others, we would tell them. I'm so glad that someone was brave enough to tell me that I was wrong about Islam. It was a painful shot in the arm that I needed, and later I recognized it as God's saving grace.

Most Muslims believe they are following God, but they are ignorant of the truth about God. The Bible says in John 1:18, *No one has seen God at any time. The only begotten Son who is in the bosom of the Father has declared (revealed) Him.*

It is impossible to know God apart from His Son Jesus Christ. Some people say, "I just believe in God." But who is this God? What is His name? How can we get in touch with Him? How can we go near Him? The Bible says in 1 John 5:11-12, *And this is the testimony: that God has given us eternal life, and this life is in His Son. He who has the Son has life; he who does not have the Son of God does not have life.*

Muslims cannot know the true God unless they come to Jesus Christ. We need to preach to them the Gospel of our Lord Jesus.

When you meet Muslims, you need to show them the love of God, but at the same time, you must be upfront with them. Be bold and speak with conviction. Many main line denominations try to reach out to muslims only by helping them and giving them the things they need without even telling them about Jesus and explaining to them the plan of salvation. The Bible says: " faith comes by hearing and hearing the wWord of God." Romans 10:17. We speak the truth in love with actions accompanied.

If you don't be bold and don't share the Gospel then they will think you are trying to lure and convert them, and it will have a backlash. Muslims like people who are resolute about their faith, to the point that they express it at any cost. They will see that you actually believe what you preach. Some Christians are cautious and don't mention Jesus.

We must speak the truth in love. I have witnessed to many Muslims, and by God's grace, many of them have accepted the Lord Jesus as their Savior. Muslims are shocked when they learn that I was a Muslim who converted to the Christian faith. They always want to know why. I share my testimony with power and humility, emphasizing my faith in Lord Jesus. You cannot be afraid to share the Gospel with people, especially Muslims. Otherwise, they will see you as a coward and wimp, and no Muslim wants to believe a wimp. They are looking for a genuine, pure, and honest faith that they have not experienced before.

Moreover, as Christians, regardless of whom we share the Gospel with, we must bear in mind what Paul said in 2 Timothy 1:7, *"For God has not given us a spirit of fear, but of power and of love and of a sound mind."*

There is no "formula" for sharing the Gospel, but I believe the best way is to be led by the Holy Spirit, whose word encourages and empowers believers, and convicts unbelievers. It's important to be filled with the Holy Spirit when you share Jesus.

First, we need to know the Gospel, which is the death, burial and resurrection of Jesus Christ our Lord.

> 1 Corinthians 15:1-5
> *Moreover, brethren, I declare to you the gospel which I preached to you, which also you received and in which you stand, by which also you are saved, if you hold fast that word which I preached to you—unless you believed in vain. For I delivered to you first of all that which I also received: that Christ died for our sins according to the Scriptures, and that He was buried, and that He rose again the third day according to the Scriptures, and that He was seen by Cephas, then by the twelve.*

When Paul wrote this chapter of Corinthians, there were many eyewitnesses of Jesus' resurrection. More than five hundred people saw the risen Jesus. In addition, we can experience the power of His resurrection daily. Every answered prayer is the result of His resurrection. Make sure that you share this important truth.

The greatest struggle that Muslims have is understanding trinity. How can Jesus be God?! I had the same struggle when I heard the Gospel but when by faith I asked Jesus to help me, I felt His power and glory although I didn't know anything about trinity. His love was so overwhelming that was undeniable. Later on the Holy Spirit revealed to me what trinity is. It's a mystery and only the Holy Spirit can reveal it to us. When we say:

"Jesus is God, it doesn't mean that man is God but the other way around, God came in the flesh in the likeness of a Man.

What do we mean when was say: "Jesus is God."? Jesus Himself said: "The Father and I are one." John 10:30. The first verse in the Bible is:" In the beginning God created the heavens and the earth." Genesis 1:1. The word for "God" in this verse is "Elohim" in Hebrew language. It's a plural form of "El" which means "God" in Hebrew. God is one most Holy, Pure, most Powerful, all wise, all knowing and Love Nature. Three persons have this nature: the Father, The Word, The Holy Spirit. All three are Spirits and are God independently. Not that we have multiple Gods but one Nature in three Persons. They have been together from the beginning, before the foundation of the world. John 1:1-5. The "Word" came as a Man to be a sacrifice and offering for sin and we know Him as Jesus. I'm Hebrew the "JESUS" is Yashua which means "Yahweh Saves". So Jesus is the same Yahweh of the Old Testament who came into the flesh.

The following is an example of how I approach people. In the conversation, I try to keep the ball in my quarter corner. That is, I talk about the Gospel as much as possible and avoid arguments and discussions about Islam.

I met Mohammad, who was a Muslim, at his restaurant, and our conversation went on as follows:

Me: Hi, how are you?

Mohammad: Hi, I'm fine, thank you. How are you?

Me: I'm fine by God's grace, thank you. By the way, my name is Ramin.

Mohammad: My name is Mohammad. Nice meeting you.

Me: Me too. Where are you from?

Mohammad: I'm

from Shiraz. (A city in the southern part of Iran)

Me: Oh how nice, how long have you been here?

Mohammad: It's been a year.

Me: How about your family?

Mohammad: They are back in Iran.

Me: Oh, I'm sure you have missed them.

Mohammad: Oh yes, very much. I miss my son a lot.

Me: I hope you can see them soon.

Mohammad: I hope so too.

Me: May God help you.

Mohammad: Thank you.

Me: By the way, do you believe in God?

Mohammad: Yes, I'm a Muslim. I believe in Allah.

Me: I was a Muslim before, but in 2005 I gave my heart to Jesus.

Mohammad: Really? You mean you are a Christian now?

Me: Yes, sir.

Mohammad: What happened? Why did you become a Christian?

Me: Well it's a long but lovely story. Jesus really changed my life.

Mohammad: But Prophet Muhammad is the last prophet. We all must believe in him.

Me: Well this is what we have been told, but it's not true.

Mohammad: How come? Why do you say that?

Me: Well, from childhood they were telling us these things. But it doesn't mean it's the truth. What if you were born in India? Then you would have been a Hindu! Right?

Mohammad: Yes, but the Quran says that Muhammad is the last prophet and we all should believe in him.

Me: You know, God never made religion. He is not interested in religion. He desires a relationship with people. Religion is man-made, man's efforts trying to find God or earn salvation. But God's plan of salvation is different. We all have sinned and His plan was to send Jesus to die for our sins as a sacrifice, so anybody who believes in Him would be saved. It's not through what we do, but by faith in Jesus and what He has done.

Mohammad: We believe in Jesus. We love Jesus, but he was one of the major prophets. He was a very good prophet. He loved children and we Muslims seem to love Jesus more than Christians do.

Me: Well, the Bible says Jesus wasn't merely a prophet. He indeed served as a prophet, but He is the Son of God. He is God who came as a man and died for us, and three days later He rose from the dead.

Mohammad: Jesus is the Son of God??!! Quran says God doesn't have a son. How can God have a Son? You mean He had a wife?

Me: Certainly not. When the Bible says God's Son, it doesn't mean God married a woman to have a son, that's a wrong conception. In Greek, the word son means one who can fully exhibit His Father's character. Jesus was the only person who could fully manifest God's character. When we say He is the Son of God, it is in that sense. Jesus wasn't a created being, but He was with God from the beginning along with the Holy Spirit. His name was the Word of God. These three have been together from the beginning and have one common nature. All three are God, they are three persons but one Holy nature. So God is one in quality but three persons. God's plan was to change our hearts. He prepared the world for the coming of the Savior.

Mohammad: But Jesus prophesied about the coming of Prophet Muhammad.

Me: That's not true. Jesus, in fact, talked about false prophets who will come and deceive many. Nowhere in my Bible does it say that Muhammad is a prophet.

Mohammad: But the Bible has been changed.

Me: Is there proof? There is no evidence of the Bible being distorted. These are lies perpetuated by the enemies of the Gospel. See, God is wise. He didn't give the entire Bible to one person, but He gave different segments of the scripture to different prophets in different times of history. Each time God gave a portion of the scripture to one of the prophets, it would be copied and everybody had a copy and the same thing happened to every portion of the Bible. For someone to change it, he must gather all the copies and change all of them, which is virtually impossible to do.

Mohammad: So you mean the Quran is not God's word?

Me: Correct. It cannot be because what the Quran says contradicts what the Bible says, so it cannot be from the same source. The Bible says that God gave His Son as a sacrifice for sin and the Quran completely denies that, so both cannot be from the same God.

Mohammad: What about the Prophet Muhammad?

Me: Muhammad wasn't a prophet from God. All of the prophets were Jewish because God had a covenant only with the Jewish people. They all prophesied about the coming of the Savior. All of them were in harmony. They didn't contradict each other or discredit the writings of preceding prophets. Muhammad wasn't a Jew, yet he contradicted the writing of the Jewish prophets and discredited the writings of other prophets by saying that they were distorted. And rationally, it couldn't be. Muhammad didn't bring any solution to man's problem. We already had the Law of Moses, which consisted of 613 laws and perfect in its kind, but it cannot save us. Muhammad also invented a kind of law, which is unable to save humanity. For example, the Quran says you have to pray five times a day. But have you really prayed faithfully and done everything that Islam has asked you to do?

Mohammad: Not really, but I have done my best.

Me: So will the best you have done save you?

Mohammad: I'm not sure. Allah knows.

Me: What if it doesn't?

Mohammad: We just do what we can and Allah is merciful?

Me: If he is merciful, why then are you not sure? Either it's his mercy or your works.

Mohammad: On judgment day, Allah will examine our works, and if our good works exceed our bad works, then we go to heaven. If not, then we go to hell and pay for our sins. Then eventually we will go to heaven.

Me: But the Bible says there is no way out of hell once you go there. Plus you never know how many good works are enough. Jesus said, "He who believes in me, I will raise him up on the last day." He said, "He who believes in me shall not taste death" (eternal death)." God loved you so much that He gave His Son to die in your place.

Mohammad: But I'm not sure that's the truth.

Me: See, Jesus said we would know a tree by its fruit. Look at lives Jesus has changed, including mine. I was a bad person, but since Jesus has come into my heart, I'm not the same old person. I know it. Look at the way Jesus lived. He never drew a sword, killed anybody, or went to war. He never committed any sin. He asked us to forgive our enemies, love them, and pray for them. Other religious leaders violently fought, murdered, and had many wives. Jesus is a better person to follow. You inherited your faith from your ancestors. It was imposed on you. But today you can choose your eternity. God will forgive all your sins. He gives you a new life, and in this world, He will help and protect you. All He wants is your genuine faith. Put your trust in Jesus. Do you want to receive Him?

Mohammad: Yes, I want to.

Mohammad gave His heart to Jesus, and a few months later, he was baptized. Not all people we that we witness to will accept the Lord on the first day, but we need to sow a seed into their heart through which the Holy Spirit can work in them. I know some Muslims who accepted the Lord eight years after they first heard the Gospel. It depends on how ready they are, which country they are from, and from what background and culture they come. Paul the Apostle said in 1 Corinthians 3:6: "*I planted, Apollos watered, but **God gave the increase**"*. Never be discouraged if they say no. Remember, our job is not to convert them. Our job is to share the truth of the Gospel in love and leave the rest in the hands of the Holy Spirit. At the end of every conversation, ask them if they need prayer and if they want to receive the Lord Jesus.

Muslims come from a shame culture, they come from a social and tribal thinking, and usually they consider their whole family and tribe before making a decision. It's better to share the Gospel with them individually and in private. In front of the rest of the family, they are afraid or ashamed to open their hearts. Unconditional love is important. Muslims have always been touched by the love of Christians. They never had that love, so show them love. Take them out for lunch or coffee. Pray and intercede for them. They are touched when they see we pray before our meals. Little things like that can move them.

Chapter Twenty

FROM ASHES TO GLORY

As described in previous chapters, the Persian Empire was arguably the greatest empire that ever existed. It created the most astonishing piece of engineering the world had ever seen at the time –magnificent palaces that rose from barren deserts, roadways, bridges, and canals. Unrelenting, fearless, and formidable, the scale of this gigantic empire extended from North Africa to Asia. It was an empire unlike any other in riches, great culture, and innovation. The extraordinary and ambitious rulers of this all-powerful civilization wrote the first human rights declaration. Yet it hasn't seen the face of peace and human rights since the Islamic revolution and takeover in 1979.

The citizens of Iran thought that Islam's reign would bring about peace and justice, but they were deceived. The selfishness of mullahs and their false promises of free gas, water and oil money brought nothing but bloodshed, pain and destruction. Those who think and believe differently from Muslims count as infidels and enemies of Islam and the revolution. Iran has had the highest number of executions, stoning, imprisonment, and torture of any nation.

After the disputed election of Mahmoud Ahmadinejad in 2009, many people who protested their stolen votes were killed. The death of a student, Nedā Āghā-Soltān, garnered global attention after she was fatally shot in the heart as she walked back to her car from the protests.

Bystanders captured her death on video and streamed it live over the Internet. During that time, Basij, a para-military Islamic group, fought people on the streets and many young people were later raped in jail. Today, seventy percent of Iranians are under the age of thirty, most of whom are educated, open-minded, and with God-given gifts and talents. But they are in a colossal jail, and that jail is Iran.

Presently more than five million Iranians are scattered around the world, and political leaders and human rights activists remain incarcerated. Many Iranian teens have been either thrown in jail or executed for political and religious reasons.

Many of those who were responsible for or had a part in the Islamic revolution have been remorseful. It didn't take long before they began to pay for what they had done, with their blood and that of their children. The same people who said, "The devil left and the angel came," then said, "Death to us who said death to the Shah," but it was too late. To this day, they are still paying for it. Indeed, many who reminisce the pre-revolution era are grieved and ask themselves, 'What have we done?' Many Iranians are ashamed of what their country has become, a sponsor and hotbed of terrorism.

Even as I write this book, many Iran are in prison for their Christian faith or for holding opinions different from the Islamic rulers. Many Christians in underground churches have been arrested in the past decades, and their leaders killed by the Islamic regime. Pastors have laid down their lives for the sake of the Gospel and the Church. I personally know three women whose husbands were killed in Iran because they were active pastors who had converted from Islam.

It's my belief that Islamic countries are not ready for democracy because it proceeds out of changed hearts that are capable of practicing mutual respect, tolerance and acceptance of others despite differences in belief systems, as long as they don't harm others or the frame of society. In contrast, Islam wants supremacy and therefore, intolerant of opposing views. It wants to rule the world and anything or anyone that's a hindrance is an enemy. That's why democracy doesn't happen or last in Islamic countries. If there is a moderate Muslim in power, soon he will be perceived as a counterfeit follower of Islam, and brought down by Muslims. This is exactly what happened to the Shah of Iran, President Mubarak of Egypt, former Egyptian leader Anwar Sadat of Egypt, and many other such examples throughout history.

Unless the people's hearts are changed by the Gospel, we will never see democracy in Muslim lands.

GOD'S PLAN FOR IRAN

The Lord showed me at the beginning of 2017 that the Iranian regime will soon fall, there have already been many protests and uprisings. It's like a volcano that is smoking and has the signs of an eruption. People are tired of being bullied by the Islamists. Inflation is skyrocketing. unemployment is at 12 per cent. Iran is known throughout the world not for its technological discoveries or economic achievements but for being the first sponger of terrorism. Just recently many people in various cities protest against the Islamic regime despite the dang

er of getting shot or getting arrested and tortured. There are many young people in Iran who are tired of the statues quo. People are fed up with 40 years of oppression and have nothing to lose anymore. In 2009 uprising a young woman named Neda was walking on the street and was shot by the Islamic regime and died on the spot. That incident caused an international outrage. The video went viral.

As I am writing, people are protesting on the street right now. The Islamic regime is on the verge of collapse. For years the Islamic regime played games with people, they held elections just as a show to prove the western world that they still have legitimacy. They would put a hardliner in power, after they squeezed people then they would bring a "reformer" so people had to choose between bad and worse. This is the way regime brought people to the polls and had cameras ready to show the world that people ant them. They even would bring people from villages into the capital on the anniversary of the revolution to deceive the world an image that was simply not true.

Those days are over. On December 28 2017 people came on the streets, without a leader, spontaneously in the a city the Mashahd. People were expressing their displeasure because of inflation and high costs of almost everything. This time people crossed the line and chanted: "Death to Ayatollah." and we no longer worship arabs." referring to Islam and Muhammad. Not only they rejected the regime but Islam as a whole. People also chanted "No reformer no fundamentalist, it's over." People aslo ear down the posters of Ayatollah khomeini and Khameneie.

The protests inspired other cities to rise. President Donald J Trump also rightfully express his support to the Iranian people multiple times. Unlike Barak Obama who not only didn't support people in 2009 uprising but also sent multiple letter to Ayatollah Khameneie and struck a one sided deal which only helped the regime, lifted the sanctions and sent millions in cash to only be spend in sponsoring the terrorists. But that deal didn't benefit the people at all. Thus it is the beginning of an end.

THE TRUE CHANGE

We know from studying the Old Testament and its messianic prophecies that most Jews in the time of Jesus anticipated the coming of a messiah who would rescue them from the evil Roman oppressors by leading a violent military uprising. However, Jesus did not buy into the nationalistic rhetoric of the time. Make no mistake. He did come to save the Jews and He was indeed the Messiah, but His "rescue plan" was far from what the people had in mind. Instead of organizing an army and strategizing for war and a violent overthrow of the government, Jesus taught and demonstrated that unconditional love, non-violence, meekness, and obedience to God's will were the road to true peace and freedom. Rather than incite anarchy, He served the poor, healed the sick, calmed storms, performed miracles including raising the dead.

Jesus confirmed His non-violent stance when the soldiers came to arrest Him and one of his disciples, Simon Peter, drew a sword to defend Him. But Jesus said to Peter in Matthew 26:52: *"Put your sword in its place, for all who take the sword will perish by the sword."* It was the time to defend Himself and fight, but Jesus acted according to His nature and yielded to what He knew was God's purpose for His life.

Some would describe Middle Eastern nations of today as archaic and stuck in the barbaric ways of ages past. Indeed, most countries in that part of the world have not moved away from a culture of death and war. However, as explained previously, the propensity for violence and evil is inherent in every man and woman. We might be able to temporarily have some relative peace but No passage of time, no amount of education or material wealth or technological advancement or government leadership or drugs or some "new age mass awakening" will cure our brokenness and the world's ills. A true change of heart in every person is what's required to love properly, and no figure in history modeled love more clearly, powerfully and perfectly than Christ Himself. It's in accepting Jesus as our personal Savior that the Holy Spirit begins His work in and through us, so we may be transformed, and become like Jesus in His love for the Father.

The sorrow among today's Iranians is deeply felt. Most of them want to restore the nation to its ancient days of glory, but God's plan for them is the good news of the Gospel of Jesus Christ.

God is doing a marvelous work in Iran as millions of Persians everywhere are receiving the Lord. In Iran, underground churches are growing rapidly. People who accept Jesus have a great zeal for God. They love Jesus and are ready to pay any price for following Him. They gather in underground churches in homes. They can be arrested any time, but they continue to risk their lives and safety. They have such an intimacy with the Lord.

God is changing Iran from within. In the past few decades, many Christians have lost their lives for the sake of the Gospel. Almost twenty pastors and church leaders have been executed for their faith. This is how Christians live in other parts of the globe. Sometimes their only companion is a Bible, if they are blessed enough to have one. Many if not most Christians in Iran don't have access to a church and fellowship. They are the ones who have denied themselves, picked up their crosses, and are following Jesus. As the Bible says concerning the Martyrs in the book of Revelation 12:11: *"And they overcame him by the blood of the Lamb and by the word of their testimony, and they didn't love their lives to the death."* Let's remember them in our prayers.

The glory will return to Persia, but this time a different kind of glory…a heavenly glory. A spiritual revolution is taking place in Persia as evidenced by multitudes of Muslims converting to Christianity. A great and marvelous light will be seen not only in Persia, but also in China, Africa and many other places.

May people everywhere see the truth and serve the one true Lord and King, Jesus Christ of Nazareth, as we await His imminent return. One of these days, the whole world and its powers and glories will come to an end, and Jesus will appear in the sky. Until then, let's pray for a desperate and needy world, for each other, and share the love of God. Let's proclaim what Jesus has done for us all.

I remember the Words of Isaiah that prophesied about Jesus and His ministry.

> "The Spirit of the Lord God *is* upon Me,
> Because the Lord has anointed Me
> To preach good tidings to the poor;
> He has sent Me to heal the brokenhearted,

> To proclaim liberty to the captives,
> And the opening of the prison to *those who are* bound;
> To proclaim the acceptable year of the Lord,
> And the day of vengeance of our God;
> To comfort all who mourn,
> To console those who mourn in Zion,
> To give them beauty for ashes,
> The oil of joy for mourning,
> The garment of praise for the spirit of heaviness;
> That they may be called trees of righteousness,
> The planting of the Lord, that He may be glorified."
> Isaiah 61:1-3.

I also remember the Words of Isaiah as he prophesied about the Glory of the Lord, when he compares the glory and the beauty of man as grass that withers but the glory that God has for us and every nation is His own everlasting glory:

> "Every valley shall be exalted
> And every mountain and hill brought low;
> The crooked places shall be made straight
> And the rough places smooth;
> The glory of the Lord shall be revealed,
> And all flesh shall see *it* together;
> For the mouth of the Lord has spoken." Isaiah 40:4-5.

Finally, John spoke of the comfort that the Lord Jesus will bring to this world: "And God will wipe away **every tear** from their eyes; there shall be no more death, nor sorrow, nor crying. There shall be no more pain, for the former things have passed away." Revelation 21:4.

Iran is experiencing a true change and receiving an eternal glory in the midst of all chaos that is talking place. God is saving the sons and daughters of Cyrus the Great through the Gospel of Jesus Christ. Just as the Bible says:

"For whom He foreknew, He also predestined *to be* conformed to the image of His Son, that He might be the firstborn among many brethren. Moreover whom He predestined, these He also called; whom He called, these He also justified; and whom He justified, these He also glorified." Romans 8:29-30.

Thus, Iran is rising from Ashes to a heavenly and divine glory. The glory of being transformed to a child of God.

Amen

Chapter Twenty-One

CHRIST'S HOPE

"I have come that they may have life, and that
they may have it more abundantly."
- John 10:10

Jesus is Life and the giver of life. Unlike the world's ordinary definition of hope that "wishes or desires" for something good in the future, Biblical hope is a *"confident expectation"* for something good in the future. This bold confidence and assurance come from resting in Jesus' finished work on the cross, and in trusting that God will do as He says based on Scripture. As He has demonstrated throughout the ages, God has a pristine track record of faithfulness and keeping His promises to His people.

The Cross of Jesus Christ is where God paid the debt we couldn't pay, carried the burden we couldn't carry. He paid for our sins so we could be reconciled to our creator. Come to the Cross today and you will find your way Home. God is waiting, He is eager for people to come to Him to be forgiven, renewed, restored, refreshed and saved. The Cross of Jesus is where Salvation was provided and there no any other way. The BIBLE SAYS: "Now all things *are* of God, who has reconciled us to Himself through Jesus Christ, and has given us the ministry of reconciliation, that is, that God was in Christ reconciling the world to Himself, not imputing their trespasses to them, and has committed to us the word of reconciliation.

I love what Rev. Billy Graham once said: "Take me to the Cross, I will find my way Home from there." Home is where we are with our heavenly Father, where we have comfort, warmth, love, peace and joy that the world will not be able to give us. If you have tried everything in the world and still are empty and hopeless, come to Jesus today. There are m any young children that never experienced the love of a father. They are a fatherless generation, but the good news is that God is our Father. He loves us.

What does it mean to have an abundant life in Jesus? In John 17:1-5 Jesus said: "Jesus spoke these words, lifted up His eyes to heaven, and said: "Father, the hour has come. Glorify Your Son, that Your Son also may glorify You, as You have given Him authority over all flesh, that He should[a] give eternal life to as many as You have given Him. And this is eternal life, that they may know You, the only true God, and Jesus Christ whom You have sent. I have glorified You on the earth. I have finished the work which You have given Me to do. And now, O Father, glorify Me together with Yourself, with the glory which I had with You before the world was."

It means that as result of Jesus' obedience on the Cross, the curse is broken off the lives of those who believe. It means wholeness in every aspect of our lives, in our relationships, health, careers, etc. After all, "He who did not spare His own Son, but delivered Him up for us all, how shall He not with Him also freely give us all things?" Romans 8:32.

When I was a Muslim, I was in perpetual shame and guilt; frankly, I didn't like myself because I attached my worth and identity to a false and dead-end religion. I was so distraught and didn't believe that my life amounted to anything. I reached a point where ending it was the only path that made sense. I had given up on myself, but clearly God had other plans for my life, and because I humbled myself and called upon Jesus to look upon my brokenness with kindness and mercy, He drew me to Himself. Today, nothing gives me more joy than serving Jesus and His Church, and sharing Him with others.

> Jeremiah 29:11
> *For I know the thoughts that I think toward you, says the* Lord, *thoughts of peace and not of evil, to give you a future and a hope.*

We have a good and all-powerful God who still heals and restores (because the Bible says, "Jesus Christ is the same yesterday, today, and forever."), but Jesus Himself said we would face trials and hardship in this world. I came to realize that the point of the Christian faith is not always to fully answer life's most challenging questions, or to eliminate events of pain and suffering from our lives, but to have joy and peace in spite of them, to find meaning in them, just as Jesus' suffering and death had meaning (of epic proportions!). Christians, therefore, are not exempt from suffering; in fact, Jesus calls us to take up cross and follow Him (Matthew 16:24).

> Paul says in Romans 1:3:
> *And not only that, but we also glory in tribulations, knowing that tribulation produces perseverance, and perseverance, character; and character, hope. Now hope does not disappoint, because the love of God has been poured out in our hearts by the Holy Spirit who was given to us."*

> Jesus said in John 16:33:
> *"These things I have spoken to you, that in Me you may have peace. In the world you will have tribulation; but be of good cheer, I have overcome the world."*

What sets Christianity apart from other faiths is that the battle has already been won. We need not struggle anymore. We can rest easy knowing that no matter how difficult things get along the way, we are assured of victory in Jesus, and that we have been adopted into God's family with whom we are to spend eternity. We know how the story ends…in victory.

Therefore, I want to encourage you today. Nothing that you may be struggling with is beyond God's power to turn around. It doesn't matter where you have fallen or how deep you are in ashes, there is hope in Jesus. You can rise by His grace. God's hand is not short to reach you and raise you, as He did me when I was in despair.

As the song goes:

> "You raised me up, so I can stand on mountains.
> You raised me up to walk on stormy seas.
> I'm strong when I'm on your shoulders.
> You raised me up to more than I can be."

You may have been hurt, rejected, mocked or despised, but know that there is one who is closer than a brother and loves you unconditionally. God's desire is for you to know Him intimately through Jesus.

> 2 Corinthians 12:9
> "My grace is sufficient for you, for My strength is made perfect in weakness…"

Therefore, I want to leave and send you with Christ's words:

> John 14:27
> "Peace I leave with you, My peace I give to you; not as the world gives do I give to you. Let not your heart be troubled, neither let it be afraid."

> Jesus is Alpha snd Omega, the beginning and the end.
> Jesus is Lord.

QURAN'S VIOLANT VERSES

Please note that the word "fight" is "kill" in original Arabic text.

Quran (2:191-193) - *"And kill them wherever you find them, and*

turn them out from where they have turned you out. And Al-Fitnah [disbelief or unrest] *is worse than killing... but if they desist, then lo! Allah is forgiving and merciful. And fight them until there is no more Fitnah* [disbelief and worshipping of others along with Allah] *and worship is for Allah alone. But if they cease, let there be no transgression except against Az-Zalimun(the polytheists, and wrong-doers, etc.)"'fighting'* is sanctioned even if the *fitna* 'ceases'. This is about religious order, not real persecution.]

Quran (2:244) - *"Then fight in the cause of Allah, and know that Allah Heareth and knoweth all things."*

Quran (2:216) - *"***Fighting is prescribed for you,*** and ye dislike it. But it is possible that ye dislike a thing which is good for you, and that ye love a thing which is bad for you. But Allah knoweth, and ye know not."* Not only does this verse establish that violence can be virtuous, but it also contradicts the myth that fighting is intended only in self-defense, since the audience was obviously not under attack at the time. From the Hadith, we know that this verse was narrated at a time that Muhammad was actually trying to motivate his people into raiding merchant caravans for loot.

Quran (3:56) - *"As to those who reject faith, I will punish them with terrible agony in this world and in the Hereafter, nor will they have anyone to help."*

Quran (3:151) - *"Soon shall We cast terror into the hearts of the Unbelievers, for that they joined companions with Allah, for which He had sent no authority"*. This speaks directly of polytheists, yet it also includes Christians, since they believe in the Trinity (ie. what Muhammad incorrectly believed to be 'joining companions to Allah').

Quran (4:74) - *"Let those fight in the way of Allah who sell the life of this world for the other. Whoso fighteth in the way of Allah, be he slain or be he victorious, on him We shall bestow a vast reward."* The martyrs of Islam are unlike the early Christians, who were led meekly to the slaughter. These Muslims are killed in battle as they attempt to inflict death and destruction for the cause of Allah. This is the theological basis for today's suicide bombers.

Quran (4:76) - *"Those who believe fight in the cause of Allah..."*

Quran (4:89) - *"They but wish that ye should reject Faith, as they do, and thus be on the same footing (as they): But take not friends from their ranks until they flee in the way of Allah (From what is forbidden). But if they turn renegades, seize them and slay them wherever ye find them; and (in any case) take no friends or helpers from their ranks."*

Quran (4:95) - *"Not equal are those of the believers who sit (at home), except those who are disabled (by injury or are blind or lame, etc.), and those who strive hard and fight in the Cause of Allah with their wealth and their lives. Allah has preferred in grades those who strive hard and fight with their wealth and their lives above those who sit (at home).Unto each, Allah has promised good (Paradise), but Allah has preferred those who strive hard and fight, above those who sit (at home) by a huge reward "* This passage criticizes "peaceful" Muslims who do not join in the violence, letting them know that they are less worthy in Allah's eyes. It also demolishes the modern myth that "Jihad" doesn't mean holy war in the Quran, but rather a spiritual struggle. Not only is this Arabic word (mujahiduna) used in this passage, but it is clearly *not* referring to anything spiritual, since the physically disabled are given exemption. (The Hadith reveals the context of the passage to be in response to a blind man's protest that he is unable to engage in Jihad, which would not make sense if it meant an internal struggle).

Quran (4:104) - *"And be not weak hearted in pursuit of the enemy; if you suffer pain, then surely they (too) suffer pain as you suffer pain..."* Is pursuing an injured and retreating enemy really an act of self-defense?

Quran (5:33) - *"The punishment of those who wage war against Allah and His messenger and strive to make mischief in the land is only this, that they should be murdered or crucified or their hands and their feet should be cut off on opposite sides or they should be imprisoned; this shall be as a disgrace for them in this world, and in the hereafter they shall have a grievous chastisement"*

Quran (8:12) - *"(Remember) when your Lord inspired the angels... "I will cast terror into the hearts of those who disbelieve. Therefore strike off their heads and strike off every fingertip of them"* No reasonable person would interpret this to mean a spiritual struggle, given that it both followed and preceded confrontations in which non-Muslims were killed by Muslims. The targets of violence are *"those who disbelieve"* - further defined in the next verse (13) as those who *"defy and disobey Allah."* Nothing is said about self-defense. In fact, the verses in sura 8 were narrated shortly after a battle provoked by Muhammad, who had been trying to attack a lightly-armed caravan to steal goods belonging to other people.

Quran (8:15) - *"O ye who believe! When ye meet those who disbelieve in battle, turn not your backs to them. (16)Whoso on that day turneth his back to them, unless maneuvering for battle or intent to join a company, he truly hath incurred wrath from Allah, and his habitation will be hell, a hapless journey's end."*

Quran (8:39) - *"And fight with them until there is no more fitna* (disorder, unbelief) *and religion is all for Allah"* Some translations interpret "fitna" as "persecution", but the traditional understanding of this word is not supported by the historical context (See notes for 2:193). The Meccans were simply refusing Muhammad access to their city during the pilgrimage. Other Muslims were allowed to travel there - but not as an armed group, since Muhammad had declared war on Mecca prior to his eviction. The Meccans were also acting in defense of their religion, as it was Muhammad's intention to destroy their idols and establish Islam by force (which he later did). Hence the critical part of this verse is to fight until *"religion is only for Allah"*, meaning that the true justification of violence was the unbelief of the opposition. According to the Sira (Ibn Ishaq/Hisham 324) Muhammad further explains that *"Allah must have no rivals."*

Quran (8:57) - *"If thou comest on them in the war, deal with them so as to strike fear in those who are behind them, that haply they may remember."*

Quran (8:67) - *"It is not for a Prophet that he should have prisoners of war until he had made a great slaughter in the land..."*

Quran (8:59-60) - *"And let not those who disbelieve suppose that they can outstrip (Allah's Purpose). Lo! they cannot escape. Make ready for them all thou canst of (armed) force and of horses tethered, that thereby ye may dismay the enemy of Allah and your enemy."* As Ibn Kathir puts it in his tafsir on this passage, "Allah commands Muslims to prepare for war against disbelievers, as much as possible, according to affordability and availability."

Quran (8:65) - *"O Prophet, exhort the believers to fight..."*

Quran (9:5) - *"So when the sacred months have passed away, then slay the idolaters wherever you find them, and take them captive and besiege them and lie in wait for them in every ambush, then if they repent and keep up prayer and pay the poor-rate, leave their way free to them."* According to this verse, the best way of staying safe from Muslim violence at the time of Muhammad was to convert to Islam: prayer (*salat*) and the poor tax (*zakat*) are among the religion's Five Pillars. The popular claim that the Quran only inspires violence within the context of self-defense is seriously challenged by this passage as well, since the Muslims to whom it was written were obviously not under attack. Had they been, then there would have been no waiting period (earlier verses make it a duty for Muslims to fight in self-defense, even during the sacred months). The historical context is Mecca *after* the idolaters were subjugated by Muhammad and posed no threat. Once the Muslims had power, they violently evicted those unbelievers who would not convert.

[Note: The verse says to fight unbelievers *"wherever you find them"*. Even if the context is a time of battle (which it was not) the reading appears to sanction attacks against those "unbelievers" who are not on the battlefield. In 2016, the Islamic State referred to this verse in urging the faithful to commit terror attacks: *Allah did not only command the 'fighting' of disbelievers, as if to say He only wants us to conduct frontline operations against them. Rather, He has also ordered that they be slain wherever they may be – on or off the battlefield.* (source)]

Quran (9:14) - *"Fight against them so that Allah will punish them by your hands and disgrace them and give you victory over them and heal the breasts of a believing people."* Humiliating and hurting non-believers not only has the blessing of Allah, but it is ordered as a means of carrying out his punishment and even "heals" the hearts of Muslims.

Quran (9:20) - *"Those who believe, and have left their homes and striven with their wealth and their lives in Allah's way are of much greater worth in Allah's sight. These are they who are triumphant."* The Arabic word interpreted as "striving" in this verse is the same root as "Jihad". The context is obviously holy war.

Quran (9:29) - *"Fight those who believe not in Allah nor the Last Day, nor hold that forbidden which hath been forbidden by Allah and His*

Messenger, nor acknowledge the religion of Truth, (even if they are) of the People of the Book, until they pay the Jizya with willing submission, and feel themselves subdued." "People of the Book" refers to Christians and Jews. According to this verse, they are to be violently subjugated, with the sole justification being their religious status. Verse 9:33 tells Muslims that Allah has charted them to make Islam "superior over all religions." This chapter was one of the final "revelations" from Allah and it set in motion the tenacious military expansion, in which Muhammad's companions managed to conquer two-thirds of the Christian world in the next 100 years. Islam is intended to dominate all other people and faiths.

Quran (9:30) - *"And the Jews say: Ezra is the son of Allah; and the Christians say: The Messiah is the son of Allah; these are the words of their mouths; they imitate the saying of those who disbelieved before; may Allah destroy them; how they are turned away!"*

Quran (9:38-39) - *"O ye who believe! what is the matter with you, that, when ye are asked to go forth in the cause of Allah, ye cling heavily to the earth? Do ye prefer the life of this world to the Hereafter? But little is the comfort of this life, as compared with the Hereafter. Unless ye go forth, He will punish you with a grievous penalty, and put others in your place."* This is a warning to those who refuse to fight, that they will be punished with Hell. The verse also links physical fighting to the "cause of Allah" (or "way of Allah").

Quran (9:41) - *"Go forth, light-armed and heavy-armed, and strive with your wealth and your lives in the way of Allah! That is best for you if ye but knew."* See also the verse that follows (9:42) - *"If there had been immediate gain (in sight), and the journey easy, they would (all) without doubt have followed thee, but the distance was long, (and weighed) on them"* This contradicts the myth that Muslims are to fight only in self-defense, since the wording implies that battle will be waged a long distance from home (in another country and - in this case - on Christian soil, according to the historians).

Quran (9:73) - *"O Prophet! strive hard against the unbelievers and the hypocrites and be unyielding to them; and their abode is hell, and evil is the destination."* Dehumanizing those who reject Islam, by reminding Muslims that unbelievers are merely firewood for Hell, makes it easier to justify slaughter. It explains why today's devout Muslims generally have little regard for those outside the faith. The inclusion of "hypocrites" (non-practicing) within the verse also contradicts the apologist's defense that the targets of hate and hostility are wartime foes, since there was never an opposing army made up of non-religious Muslims in Muhammad's time. (See also Games Muslims Play: Terrorists Can't Be Muslim Because They Kill Muslims for the role this verse plays in Islam's perpetual internal conflicts).

Quran (9:88) - *"But the Messenger, and those who believe with him, strive and fight with their wealth and their persons: for them are (all) good things: and it is they who will prosper."*

Quran (9:111) - *"Allah hath purchased of the believers their persons and their goods; for theirs (in return) is the garden (of Paradise): they fight in His cause, and slay and are slain: a promise binding on Him in truth, through the Law, the Gospel, and the Quran: and who is more faithful to his covenant than Allah? then rejoice in the bargain which ye have concluded: that is the achievement supreme."* How does the Quran define a true believer?

Quran (9:123) - *"O you who believe! fight those of the unbelievers who are near to you and let them find in you hardness."*

Quran (17:16) - *"And when We wish to destroy a town, We send Our commandment to the people of it who lead easy lives, but they transgress therein; thus the word proves true against it, so We destroy it with utter destruction."* Note that the crime is moral transgression, and the punishment is "utter destruction." (Before ordering the 9/11 attacks, Osama bin Laden first issued Americans an invitation to Islam).

Quran (18:65-81) - This parable lays the theological groundwork for honor killings, in which a family member is murdered because they brought shame to the family, either through apostasy or perceived moral indiscretion. The story (which is not found in any Jewish or Christian source) tells of Moses encountering a man with "special knowledge" who does things which don't seem to make sense on the surface, but are then justified according to later explanation. One such action is to murder a youth for no apparent reason (v.74). However, the wise man later explains that it was feared that the boy would "grieve" his parents by "disobedience and ingratitude." He was killed so that Allah could provide them a 'better' son. [Note: This parable along with verse 58:22 is a major reason that honor killing is sanctioned by Sharia. Reliance of the Traveler (Umdat al-Saliq) says that punishment for murder is not applicable when a parent or grandparent kills their offspring (o.1.12).]

Quran (21:44) - "...See they not that We gradually reduce the land (in their control) from its outlying borders? Is it then they who will win?"

Quran (25:52) - "Therefore listen not to the Unbelievers, but strive against them with the utmost strenuousness with it." - The root for Jihad is used twice in this verse - although it may not have been referring to Holy War when narrated, since it was prior to the hijra at Mecca. The "it" at the end is thought to mean the Quran. Thus the verse may have originally meant a non-violent resistance to the 'unbelievers.' Obviously, this changed with the hijra. 'Jihad' after this is almost exclusively within a violent context. The enemy is always defined as people, rather than ideas.

Quran (33:60-62) - "If the hypocrites, and those in whose hearts is a disease (evil desire for adultery, etc.), and those who spread false news among the people in Al-Madinah, cease not, We shall certainly let you overpower them, then they will not be able to stay in it as your neighbors but a little while Accursed, wherever found, they shall be seized and killed with a (terrible) slaughter." This passage sanctions slaughter (rendered as "merciless" and "horrible murder" in other translations) against three groups: hypocrites (Muslims who refuse to "fight in the way of Allah" (3:167) and hence don't act as Muslims should), those with "diseased hearts" (which include Jews and Christians 5:51-52), and "alarmists" or "agitators - those who speak out against Islam. It is worth noting that the victims are to be *sought out*, which is what today's terrorists do.

Quran (47:3-4) - *"Those who disbelieve follow falsehood, while those who believe follow the truth from their Lord... So, when you meet (fighting Jihad in Allah's Cause), those who disbelieve smite at their necks till when you have killed and wounded many of them, then bind a bond firmly (on them, i.e. take them as captives)... If it had been Allah's Will, He Himself could certainly have punished them (without you). But (He lets you fight), in order to test you, some with others. But those who are killed in the Way of Allah, He will never let their deeds be lost."* Holy war is to be pursued against those who reject Allah. The unbelievers are to be killed and wounded. Survivors are to be held captive for ransom. The only reason Allah doesn't do the dirty work himself is to to test the faithfulness of Muslims. Those who kill pass the test. (See also: 47:4 for more context)

Quran (47:35) - *"Be not weary and faint-hearted, crying for peace, when ye should be uppermost* (Shakir: "have the upper hand") *for Allah is with you,"*

Quran (48:17) - *"There is no blame for the blind, nor is there blame for the lame, nor is there blame for the sick (that they go not forth to war). And whoso obeyeth Allah and His messenger, He will make him enter Gardens underneath which rivers flow; and whoso turneth back, him will He punish with a painful doom."* Contemporary apologists sometimes claim that Jihad means 'spiritual struggle.' If so, then why are the blind, lame and sick exempted? This verse also says that those who do not fight will suffer torment in hell.

Quran (48:29) - *"Muhammad is the messenger of Allah. And those with him are hard (ruthless) against the disbelievers and merciful among themselves"* Islam is **not** about treating everyone equally. This verse tells Muslims that two very distinct standards are applied based on religious status. Also the word used for 'hard' or 'ruthless' in this verse shares the same root as the word translated as 'painful' or severe' to describe Hell in over 25 other verses including 65:10, 40:46 and 50:26..

Quran (61:4) - *"Surely Allah loves those who fight in His cause"* Religion of Peace, indeed! The verse explicitly refers to "rows" or "battle array," meaning that it is speaking of physical conflict. This is followed by (61:9), which defines the "cause": *"He it is who has sent His Messenger (Mohammed) with guidance and the religion of truth (Islam) to make it* **victorious over all religions even though the infidels may resist.***"* (See next verse, below). Infidels who resist Islamic rule are to be fought.

Quran (61:10-12) - *"O You who believe! Shall I guide you to a commerce that will save you from a painful torment. That you believe in Allah and His Messenger (Muhammad), and that you strive hard and fight in the Cause of Allah with your wealth and your lives, that will be better for you, if you but know! (If you do so) He will forgive you your sins, and admit you into Gardens under which rivers flow, and pleasant dwelling in Gardens of 'Adn- Eternity ['Adn(Edn) Paradise], that is indeed the great success."* This verse refers to physical battle waged to make Islam victorious over other religions (see verse 9). It uses the Arabic root for the word Jihad.

Quran (66:9) - *"O Prophet! Strive against the disbelievers and the hypocrites, and be stern with them. Hell will be their home, a hapless journey's end."* The root word of "Jihad" is used again here. The context is clearly holy war, and the scope of violence is broadened to include "hypocrites" - those who call themselves Muslims but do not act as such.

HADITH AND SIRA

*S*ahih Bukhari (52:177) - *Allah's Apostle said, "The Hour will not be established until you fight with the Jews, and the stone behind which a Jew will be hiding will say. "O Muslim! There is a Jew hiding behind me, so kill him."*

Sahih Bukhari (52:256) - *The Prophet... was asked whether it was permissible to attack the pagan warriors at night with the probability of exposing their women and children to danger. The Prophet replied, "They (i.e. women and children) are from them (i.e. pagans)."* In this command, Muhammad establishes that it is permissible to kill non-combatants in the process of killing a perceived enemy. This provides justification for the many Islamic terror bombings.

Sahih Bukhari (52:65) - *The Prophet said, 'He who fights that Allah's Word (Islam) should be superior, fights in Allah's Cause.* Muhammad's words are the basis for offensive Jihad - spreading Islam by force. This is how it was understood by his companions, and by the terrorists of today. (See also Sahih Bukhari 3:125)

Sahih Bukhari (52:220) - *Allah's Apostle said... 'I have been made victorious with terror'*

Sahih Bukhari (52:44) - *A man came to Allah's Apostle and said, "Instruct me as to such a deed as equals Jihad (in reward)." He replied, "I do not find such a deed."*

Abu Dawud (14:2526) - *The Prophet said, Three things are the roots of faith: to refrain from (killing) a person who utters, "There is no god but Allah" and not to declare him unbeliever whatever sin he commits, and not to excommunicate him from Islam for his any action; and jihad will be performed continuously since the day Allah sent me as a prophet...*

Abu Dawud (14:2527) - *The Prophet said: Striving in the path of Allah (jihad)* is incumbent on you along with every ruler, whether he is pious or impious

Sahih Muslim (1:33) - *the Messenger of Allah said: I have been commanded to fight against people till they testify that there is no god but Allah, that Muhammad is the messenger of Allah*

Sahih Bukhari (8:387) - *Allah's Apostle said, "I have been ordered to fight the people till they say: 'None has the right to be worshipped but Allah'. And if they say so, pray like our prayers, face our Qibla and slaughter as we slaughter, then their blood and property will be sacred to us and we will not interfere with them except legally."*

Sahih Muslim (1:30) - *"The Messenger of Allah said: I have been commanded to fight against people so long as they do not declare that there is no god but Allah."*

Sahih Bukhari (52:73) - *"Allah's Apostle said, 'Know that Paradise is under the shades of swords'."*

Sahih Bukhari (11:626) - [Muhammad said:] *"I decided to order a man to lead the prayer and then take a flame to burn all those, who had not left their houses for the prayer, burning them alive inside their homes."*

Sahih Muslim (1:149) - *"Abu Dharr reported: I said: Messenger of Allah, which of the deeds is the best? He (the Holy Prophet) replied: Belief in Allah and Jihad in His cause..."*

Sahih Muslim (20:4645) - "...He (the Messenger of Allah) did that and said: There is another act which elevates the position of a man in Paradise to a grade one hundred (higher), and the elevation between one grade and the other is equal to the height of the heaven from the earth. He (Abu Sa'id) said: What is that act? He replied: Jihad in the way of Allah! Jihad in the way of Allah!"

Sahih Muslim (20:4696) - "the Messenger of Allah (may peace be upon him) said: 'One who died but did not fight in the way of Allah nor did he express any desire (or determination) for Jihad died the death of a hypocrite.'"

Sahih Muslim (19:4321-4323) - Three hadith verses in which Muhammad shrugs over the news that innocent children were killed in a raid by his men against unbelievers. His response: "They are of them (meaning the enemy)."

Sahih Muslim (19:4294) - "Fight against those who disbelieve in Allah. Make a holy war... When you meet your enemies who are polytheists, invite them to three courses of action. If they respond to any one of these, you also accept it and withhold yourself from doing them any harm. Invite them to (accept) Islam; if they respond to you, accept it from them and desist from fighting against them... If they refuse to accept Islam, demand from them the Jizya. If they agree to pay, accept it from them and hold off your hands. If they refuse to pay the tax, seek Allah's help and fight them."

Sahih Muslim (31:5917) - "Ali went a bit and then halted and did not look about and then said in a loud voice: 'Allah's Messenger, on what issue should I fight with the people?' Thereupon he (the Prophet) said: 'Fight with them until they bear testimony to the fact that there is no god but Allah and Muhammad is his Messenger'." The pretext for attacking the peaceful farming community of Khaybar was not obvious to the Muslims. Muhammad's son-in-law Ali asked the prophet of Islam to clarify the reason for their mission to kill, loot and enslave. Muhammad's reply was straightforward. The people should be fought because they are not Muslim.

<u>Sahih Muslim (31:5918)</u> - *"I will fight them until they are like us."* Ali's reply to Muhammad, after receiving clarification that the pretext for attacking Khaybar was to convert the people (see above verse).

<u>Sahih Bukhari 2:35</u> *"The person who participates in (Holy Battles) in Allah's cause and nothing compels him do so except belief in Allah and His Apostle, will be recompensed by Allah either with a reward, or booty (if he survives) or will be admitted to Paradise (if he is killed)."*

<u>Sunan an-Nasa'i</u> (Sahih) *"Whoever dies without having fought or thought of fighting, he dies on one of the branches of hypocrisy"*

<u>Sunan Ibn Majah 24:2794</u> (Sahih) - *"I came to the Prophet and said: 'O Messenger of Allah, which Jihad is best?' He said: '(That of a man) whose blood is shed and his horse is wounded.'"* Unlike the oft-quoted "Greater/Lesser" verse pertaining to Jihad, this is judged to be authentic, and clearly establishes that the 'best' Jihad involves physical violence.

<u>Tabari 7:97</u> *The morning after the murder of Ashraf, the Prophet declared, "Kill any Jew who falls under your power."* Ashraf was a poet, killed by Muhammad's men because he insulted Islam. Here, Muhammad widens the scope of his orders to kill. An innocent Jewish businessman was then slain by his Muslim partner, merely for being non-Muslim.

<u>Tabari 9:69</u> *"Killing Unbelievers is a small matter to us"* The words of Muhammad, prophet of Islam.

<u>Tabari 17:187</u> *"'By God, our religion (din) from which we have departed is better and more correct than that which these people follow. Their religion does not stop them from shedding blood, terrifying the roads, and seizing properties.' And they returned to their former religion."* The words of a group of Christians who had converted to Islam, but realized their error after being shocked by the violence and looting committed in the name of Allah. The price of their decision to return to a religion of peace was that the men were beheaded and the woman and children enslaved by the caliph Ali.

Ibn Ishaq/Hisham 484: - *"Allah said, 'A prophet must slaughter before collecting captives. A slaughtered enemy is driven from the land. Muhammad, you craved the desires of this world, its goods and the ransom captives would bring. But Allah desires killing them to manifest the religion.'"*

Ibn Ishaq/Hisham 990: Cutting off someone's head while shouting 'Allahu Akbar' is not a 'perversion of Islam', but a tradition of Islam that began with Muhammad. In this passage, a companion recounts an episode in which he staged a surprise ambush on a settlement: *"I leapt upon him and cut off his head and ran in the direction of the camp shouting 'Allah akbar' and my two companions did likewise".*

Ibn Ishaq/Hisham 992: - *"Fight everyone in the way of Allah and kill those who disbelieve in Allah."* Muhammad's instructions to his men prior to a military raid.

Ibn Kathir (Commentary on verses 2:190-193 - *Since Jihad involves killing and shedding the blood of men, Allah indicated that these men are committing disbelief in Allah, associating with Him (in the worship) and hindering from His path, and this is a much greater evil and more disastrous than killing.* One of Islam's most respected scholars clearly believed that Jihad means physical warfare.

Saifur Rahman, The Sealed Nectar p.227-228 - *"Embrace Islam... If you two accept Islam, you will remain in command of your country; but if your refuse my Call, you've got to remember that all of your possessions are perishable. My horsemen will appropriate your land, and my Prophethood will assume preponderance over your kingship."* One of several letters from Muhammad to rulers of other countries. The significance is that the recipients were not making war or threatening Muslims. Their subsequent defeat and subjugation by Muhammad's armies was justified merely on the basis of their unbelief.

Source- The Religion of peace

ABOUT THE AUTHOR

Ramin Parsa was born and raised in Iran as a devout Muslim. Ramin Parsa's dire search for Allah fueled his stringent practice of Islam. However, a series of events and revelations led him to doubt and ultimately reject the harsh, unjust, and empty religious practices and teachings of Islam that he had embraced since childhood.

Disillusioned and deeply troubled, Ramin questioned his own life's meaning and purpose, and contemplated suicide.

Ramin was 19 when he first heard and accepted the gospel of Jesus Christ, which transformed his life. Immediately after, he felt the call to pursue and serve the God of the Bible in a meaningful way.

From Glory to Ashes and From Ashes to Glory beautifully recounts Ramin's unassailable faith journey. This book speaks to how a man's faith, identity and reason for being were diminished to ashes, but restored and raised up by God to a different kind of glory.

Ramin shares jarring details of the severe persecution he has endured since becoming a Christian, and the price that Christians continue to pay for living out their faith in dangerous Muslim-majority countries.

In his book, Ramin courageously unveils the true face of Islam and its oppressive mindset and culture in stark details. You will learn about his first-hand experience with the disquieting realities of Sharia Law and

Jihad. this book is as much a powerful testimonial as it is an urgent plea for resistance against the Islamic invasion of the West, and for protection of the Judeo-Christian freedoms and principles that we love and cherish in America.

comparing and contrasting the world impacts of Islam and Christianity over millennia, Ramin makes the case that Christianity is the only demonstrable solution to humanity's ills.This story attests to the living hope and restoration that humanity can only find in Jesus Christ.

This book is an invaluable tool that provides insight into the hearts and minds of Muslims and lays out practical advice for reaching out to them in Christ's love.

Your hearts will be stirred and your passion for the Gospel re-ignited by Ramin's story of hope and redemption.

Ramin Parsa is a world-traveling evangelist, Bible teacher, and pastor of The Good Shepherd Church in Southern California, where he currently lives.

CPSIA information can be obtained
at www.ICGtesting.com
Printed in the USA
BVHW030811270220
573505BV00001B/10